Boy

© 1971 by GAVIN CRAIG

ISBN 0 245 50601 2

First published in Great Britain in 1971 by

NAUTICAL PUBLISHING COMPANY

Nautical House, Lymington, Hampshire

*Composed in 11 on 12 pt Monotype Baskerville
and made and printed in Great Britain by*
THE CAMELOT PRESS LIMITED
LONDON AND SOUTHAMPTON

GAVIN CRAIG

Boy Aloft

Erroll Bruce
Richard Creagh-Osborne
Peter Johnson

Hon. President:
Adlard Coles

Nautical House
Lymington, Hampshire

**Nautical
Publishing
Company**

in association with George G. Harrap & Co. Ltd.,
London, Toronto, Sydney, Wellington

Dedication

To a great ship,

To Millie for her unswerving loyalty, courage, patience, hard work and abiding faith,

To those fine seamen of many ranks and race who by their example, advice and the odd blow and kick, instilled in me a respect for them and their skills and a set of professional standards as lofty as the mainmast,

To that fine master of his art, E. Ehgeborg, cook of the ship, whose glorious food fortified our bodies, uplifted our sagging spirits and will remain forever in the mind, a beautiful gluttonous memory—*sic transit gloria peasoup*,

To the medical profession throughout the world—with one eminent exception—who by their knowledge, skill, nursing and sparse explanations, cured or patched me up and pitched me headlong back into the maelstrom. Collectively they owe me a debt of gratitude in that I chose to turn my back on all that the profession had to offer,

To all distillers and brewers, legal and otherwise, whose loving careful attention to their products brings new light to tired eyes, renewed energy to exhausted bodies, relaxation, contentment and a brief happiness to hold at bay the surrounding misery,

To all competent amateur and professional composers, musicians, singers, artists and writers who by the practice of their arts lure us to float in the deep starry pools of their creation as they soothe or inflame our senses and agitate our imaginations,

my grateful thanks to all.

Contents

Contents

Acknowledgements

It is with grateful thanks that I inscribe this page to the individuals and firms who have been so very helpful with information and photographs which have erased the blurs of memory and enabled me to complete this story.

Svein Molaug, Director of the Norwegian Maritime Museum; Captain Chris Steenstrup, Oslo, Norway, author of *Four-masted Full-Rigger Lancing of Kristiania*; Captain P. A. Gruelund, Pilot of Yrasavej, Denmark; Captain Malmstein of Oslo, Norway; Captain Olafsen, Master of the third vessel to bear the name. She was the tanker *Lancing* (his father, Captain O. Olafsen, commanded the original ship in the year 1920); Peder G. Melsom, a director of Melsom & Melsom, owners of *Lancing* (Mr Melsom served in the ship as a youth, for about one year, 1919/20, first as *dekksgutt* later as *jungmann* and berthed in the fo'c'sle).

Alfred Pedersen of Ayrshire, a son of the late Captain P. Th. Pedersen; Mrs Florence Thom of Glasgow, a daughter of the ship's master; A. D. Jones, director of the French Line in London, and the unknown but very helpful individuals in the Paris Office of the Compagnie Générale Transatlantique; Contre-Amiral Marcel J. Adam of Brest; Archie Wallace, editor, and James K. Allison of the *Ardrossan & Saltcoats Herald*; Craig J. M. Carter, the editor of *Sea Breezes* and *Special Publications*; also editor of the *Journal of Commerce & Shipping Telegraph Ltd*, Liverpool.

J. & P. Coates, Ltd, Glasgow, owners of the spoolwood cargo; Donald B. MacCulloch, of Glasgow; J. H. Corner, Headmaster of Vanburgh Castle School, Blackheath, for technical translations from the French; Anita V. Mozley, the editor of *Sea Letter*, from the San Francisco Maritime Museum, California; Lloyd's Register of Shipping, London; the late Frank C. Bowen, co-editor of *Mail and Passenger Steamships of the Nineteenth Century*.

The Staff of the reading and print rooms of the National Maritime Museum at Greenwich, who are so very helpful and obliging; M. K. Stammers, Keeper of Shipping, City of Liverpool Museums; William Brown Street, for a detailed description of the *Lancing* model and generous assistance with the plans of *Pereire*; A. Raffell, Chief Draughtsman of the Blyth Dry Docks & Shipbuilding, Co. Ltd, for the courtesy and an unsuccessful search into the firm's early records; F. D. Tredrey, a director of William Blackwood & Sons, and to the unknown publisher's reader who initially found some merit in my work.

Introduction

This is the story of a boyhood first voyage in a big sailing ship, the four-masted, full-rigged ship *Lancing* of Kristiania, Norway—the fastest sailing ship in the world.

The story was written because not enough is known about this wonderful unique vessel and the men who sailed her and their life aboard her.

There were no very exciting moments during the voyage, which was nothing out of the usual run of sailing ship voyages; no fires, no collisions with icebergs or other vessels, no plague or serious accidents to ship or crew. It was just an ordinary Western Ocean voyage of a fast, powerful and well-sailed windjammer.

However, the sequence of events are not guaranteed, since the writer was only a boy and never kept a diary but relies on an excellent visual memory to augment his research.

The ship may have encountered the iceberg while bound to the eastward and not the west, while the sighting of the liner, *Baltic*, may well have taken place many days earlier or later than is indicated. The incidents described during the voyage actually took place, but where no date is given, the precise time and actual geographical location are doubtful.

GAVIN CRAIG

London.

Author's Notes

The omission of the definite article is deliberate, for no one ever used it in reference to this ship. From Captain to Cabin Boy from Consul to Clerk and all who knew her by association or reputation she was always spoken of and written about *by her name only*. Why this should be so I do not know. Perhaps it was a form of respect for a great ship.

The division of time into Watches in *Lancing* was not the same as in British ships, as will be clear from the table below. It had the advantage of a long afternoon below every other day, when an uninterrupted rest was *possible*, in fine weather. Unlike the established custom in British ships, seven bells was struck at 1130 in the morning watch, not at 1120.

Watchkeeping in *Lancing*
1230–1900
1900–2400
0001–0400
0400–0800
0800–1230

CHAPTER ONE

I Discover My Ship

Long before I reached the age of 16 and sailed in her, I knew my first ship intimately. She was a sailing ship and the very last of her rig. The last active survivor of all the four-masted, full-rigged ships ever to sail the oceans of the world, from the first *L'Invention*, a privateer of the year 1800 built at Bordeaux to the ideas of the famous Frenchman, Colbert, who had founded a school of naval architecture under Louis XIV, to this, British-built, Norwegian-owned, vessel.

She was reckoned by knowledgeable seamen, shippers and historians, to be the fastest and greatest record-holder in existence, yet few people in the British Isles had ever heard of her. However, in all the Scandanavian countries she is still remembered and spoken of with pride.

Her name was *Lancing* and she was registered in the port of Kristiania, Norway. Surprisingly, she began her long and interesting career, not as a sailing ship but as a steamer, a transatlantic passenger liner owned and managed by the Compagnie Générale Transatlantique of Le Havre, France, now known as the French Line.

I was a small, restless, dissatisfied and unhappy schoolboy aged about 13 with a head full of *Coral Island*, *Treasure Island*, *The Brass-bounder*, the tales of Jack London, of W. W. Jacobs and a host of others, when I first heard of her.

I had recently changed schools. Perhaps the Head had prevailed on my parents to give me a fighting chance elsewhere, or maybe they had collectively decided that the form of education which was offered by Glasgow Academy was beyond my assimilation. This was classical in form and was designed to prepare me for entry to a university and, later, for a professional career so that I might follow in the footsteps

13

of my father who was a Doctor of Medicine and Surgery.

Since I was the only son of a family of five children, it was impressed upon me by my mother that I would be very lucky indeed to inherit a large and lucrative practice with patients numbering several thousands, both private and panel. To my parents' credit they did not try too hard to force me to make a decision in their favour or exact a promise that I would try to become a doctor. No doubt they already knew it was useless.

My father, however, tried to germinate a spark of interest in his work by taking me on Saturday visits to his patients and sometimes I would accompany him into the house and, on rare occasions, into the sickroom. But most times I would await him in the carriage or brougham, while the driver read a newspaper or dozed on the box seat up front and the horse clanged its steel shoes on the stones of the street or nuzzled into the haybag hanging from its head.

I did not like the waiting periods of these outings and I was usually much relieved when my father returned to the carriage. As we moved away, he would relate to me a brief résumé of the patient's complaint and the treatment necessary, but only if it were fit for my tender ears.

Another method which he used to try to interest me in medicine was to prevail upon me to attend at the surgery where I would be given the job of testing urine for sugar, albumin, or something. This exercise gave me the horrors and I loathed the job. The patients brought their samples in beer bottles and sometimes in old, cracked, open jugs. The aroma and the steam from the boiling liquid, plus the splashes on my hands from the test tubes, convinced me that the practice of medicine and the art of surgery were not for me.

No one, least of all my father, knew that I was allergic to cotton wool, repelled by the sight of surgical appliances in shop windows (common at that time), of surgical instruments in glass cabinets, and the spurt and ooze of suppuration—in others.

The new abode of teaching into which I was thrust rejoiced in the title of Alan Glen's School and was smack in the centre of the city. Who Alan Glen was nobody seemed to know, certainly not the pupils, though there was a relief bust or plaque of a well-fed, hairy individual on the wall of a dark stairway which might have represented the noble being, but no one stopped to read the inscription. One hundred or so boys slowly plodded up these stairs *en masse* or tore down them at speed so the identity of the gentleman remained a mystery, except to the sculptor of course.

The pattern of education here was 'modern' and was designed to prepare the youth of the city for any trade, from ship-building to serving behind a counter. I still had to suffer instruction in French but I was no longer the victim of the Latin language.

I hated to be taught. I loathed all schools. Even the sight of a strange school anywhere caused me to turn my head away. I regarded them as punishment centres for helpless youth. Oh, I had it drummed into me that education was the only way to succeed in life, and then the next minute I would be told about some ignorant peasant, who could neither read nor write, selling newspapers in the streets as a boy and rising later to the giddy heights of great wealth.

My sketches brought me to the notice of one of my fellow-sufferers in the same form, a Danish boy named Alan Blanner, whose father was the Norwegian Vice-Consul in Glasgow. Ships were our common ground and we swopped books and magazines about the sea while discussing, in particular, sailing ships.

The way Alan put it to me when we chummed up was that his Dad owned a big sailing ship and that her name was *Lancing*. I discovered later, by a study of the initial letters on her house-flag, that the partners of a firm named Melsom & Melsom in Kristiania, Norway, were the managing owners. Mr Christian Blanner may have had an interest in the ship for all I knew, but it did not matter to me one way or the other. On a promise from Alan, I was going to be introduced to a sailing ship, in person!

I had, of course, played truant many, many times and haunted the docks, gazing, with a cracked heart which poured out a painful aching longing towards the west where the nearest ocean lay, at the sailing ships and camouflaged steamers. But it was the sailing ships that I loved with all the nerves of my diminutive body.

I liked particularly The Broomielaw on a quiet summer Sunday, when the steel clatter of horse's shoes, the creaking, squealing rumble of loaded carts, the crack of whips and swearing shouts of drivers were stilled. When the shawled women and the foreign sailors sat on steps drinking bottled beer, smoking cigarettes and spitting loudly into the gutters.

There were two shops on whose windows my nose would flatten, for beyond the glass lay the world, my world. There were hardwood fids, steel marline spikes, sheath knives, sewing palms, models of ships, of barques and of small coasting schooners, sharks' jawbones with rows of serrated teeth and walking sticks made from the backbone of this fish, whales' teeth with scrimshaw whaling pictures, tobacco pouches of albatross skin, tattered volumes with strange foreign titles in long, long words, British nautical text-books, turnip watches half-an-inch thick and complete with chains and seals, and netting needles, all in a jumbled disarray, designed to lure one into a guessing game of identifying something new and exciting with each flick of the eyes. I considered these shops to be veritable treasure houses!

It was in this district that I came upon a real character who appeared to have stepped straight out of an adventure story. He was a big negro, dressed in a loose, grey shapeless suit, but he wore real cowboy boots with high heels and on his head was a 'ten-gallon' stetson hat which had an ornamentation of plain, silvery convex discs around the band. He was not spurred but I had sidled closer, eager to see if he had a 'six-gun' in a holster hanging from his belt or maybe tucked into the waist-band of his trousers.

No weapon was visible but he wore a plaited leather belt with the embossed head of a steer on the silver buckle, while his trouser pockets did not follow the seams of the legs but slanted across the front of his stomach. I noticed that the trousers were worn outside the boot-legs. He was deeply engaged in conversation, his voice having an American accent, with a companion, a boldly handsome young woman wearing the usual black shawl over a low-cut, white, frilly blouse. Her hair and eyes were very dark and she had powder on her face. She wore silk stockings and new high-heeled black shoes. As I edged away they were laughing together. They remain still an interesting and impressive picture in the dusty warm sunlight and soft purple shadows of the old Broomielaw dock road.

My first contact with an American sailing ship was made

about this period. She was a lovely schooner with an apple-green hull, dazzling white deck-houses, oiled masts and varnished booms and gaffs, long bowsprit and jib-boom, white cross-trees, white and black standing rigging and a beautifully clean ensign floating above her white taffrail. Her officers wore uniform caps with clean white shirts and faded blue overall trousers. The stowed sails were white as new linen. Everything about her was clean and shipshape. She was yacht-like. I gave my heart to her from a distance, then approached and read her name, *Marion G. Douglas*.

Standing alongside the schooner, for she was at a river berth and had no fenders out, I stroked the scarred planks of her emerald hull, then sought to hear if she were empty by giving a hard knock to them. My knuckles were sore for hours after. Still, I did discover that the planking of a wooden ship was a great deal thicker than a house door.

A few days earlier I had been a passenger in a Clyde paddle-steamer and we had passed close to a Russian cruiser in the Gareloch. She was anchored, for I think she had been requisitioned owing to the Revolution. Her name was *Askold* and she had five funnels. The citizens of Glasgow and Greenock called her 'the packet of Woodbines'. She was dirty, had a ram-bow and guns in window-boxes along her sides, for the guns were enclosed by glass screens, presumably as harbour protection against the weather.

What a contrast it was between that Russian cruiser, the dazzle-painted merchantmen, of which one was a two-funnelled passenger liner with a hole in her port side big enough to admit a tramcar, and this sea-witch of a schooner, which looked like a lovely palm tree in a field of sugar beet.

One Saturday morning, Alan and I met at the Shell in the Central Railway Station and made our way by tramcar across the river to Govan, where *Lancing* was enshrined between timber shores in a graving dock, close to the old shipyard where she had been built in 1865. My first sight of her was thrilling. From the top platform on the front of the tramcar, long before we reached her we could see her lofty masts and yards soaring above the tall tenement dwellings wrapped in their chimneys' smoky haze. Her masts appeared to be stepped far apart while her yards seemed to occupy a great deal of space in the gloomy sky.

The twists and turns of the tramway route obscured our view of her masts or altered the perspective so that the masts and yards closed together or opened out from minute to minute. The buildings closed in on us and she was gone. Then they opened out a little and through gaps we saw her again, looming larger and larger until the tramcar turned the last corner and ran parallel with the high railings surmounting the wall of the dry docks.

We looked at her. There she was, set in the low stone dock like a gigantic model, stern on, upright in the long narrow basin, her yards braced to starboard. The black hull with the broad white band decorated with painted gun-ports showed the rust stains of her passage from New Caledonia, or perhaps it was from Santos in Brazil. I did not care where she had come from or whither she was bound, all I was interested in was *her*!

We made our way to the gate of the dockyard and boldly marched inside. A bored-looking Army sentry smelling of beer was talking to a policeman outside a small stone lodge. They glanced at the pass Alan had been given at the Consulate, nodded, then ignored our existence.

Running helter-skelter down the stone ramp we stopped at the bottom to admire her bows and upthrust bowsprit, craning our necks to gaze awe-struck aloft and burying chins in chests as we leant on the low stone wall and tried to see under her bottom. Two large stained and rust-streaked Norwegian flags were painted on her starboard side while between them in big weather-soiled white lettering the words, LANCING—NORGE, disfigured the sweep of her bulwarks.

Scampering up the heavy timber brow spanning the wide gap between dockside and ship, we ignored the inboard ladder and jumped down on to the large spare spar lashed to the bulwark stanchions then ran along it and sprang to the iron deck. Alan led the way aft to the cabin with an assurance which demonstrated a kind of proprietary interest in the vessel, or so I was induced to believe. I followed along and as I stepped over the high coaming of the cabin doorway into the quiet warmth of the alleyway, the indescribable scents of a sailing ship enveloped me—and held me forever.

There were lazy, warm, comfortable smells, some reminiscent of village grocery stores, others of a blacksmith's forge, a carpenter's shop and a boat-builder's yard. All were compounded and layered with dry cereals, cooked food, drying rope, paraffin and heated woollen blankets, tobacco and paint with the tang of gin, coffee, soap and hot biscuits, beeswax and new canvas, a coal-burning fire, hot metal, mahogany, teakwood and fresh-sawn pine. And wet rust, mildew and new-baked bread. A *pot pourri* of a smell!

The Master and Second Mate were ashore but the First Mate was present. At the sound of our voices he stepped from his room on the port side and, filling a pipe with cut tobacco from his palm, greeted Alan, whom he knew, in a strong vigorous clear voice, speaking Norwegian. I was surprised by the tones of the voice, coming from such an ancient face and stooped, frail body. He walked with a slow shuffle, dragging his feet as though there was something wrong with his legs. Later I was told that he had been badly injured in a fall from aloft in another ship.

I was introduced and the conversation carried on in English. The Mate's name was Larsen. He had very blue eyes in a tanned and weather-beaten face, the colour of which was very much darker than the well washed, unpressed patrol suit which he was wearing with the jacket unbuttoned, revealing a clean white singlet and a mass of hair reaching up to his throat. The back of his neck was crossed with many wrinkles which held my admiration, as they demonstrated that this officer was a real 'sailing ship man' who had spent a lifetime examining the sails above, the masts, the yards, the standing and running rigging and the look of the weather. I eagerly anticipated the time when the back of my neck would advertise my profession as clearly as his did!

He asked us if we would like coffee and called quietly for the steward, who shortly appeared from another cabin. He was a pale-faced, short, thickset man, aged about 40, with the big bushy moustache of the period, he wore black trousers held by narrow, coloured braces over a striped, collarless flannel shirt.

We entered the saloon, as the officer returned to his cabin, and I saw that the place was furnished with two long dining tables set on pedestals and covered with green baize table-cloths. We seated ourselves at the port table, Alan on the settee which extended the length of the room and myself in a swivel armchair, facing him.

The steward spread a section of folded white tablecloth over the end of the table and served us with delicious coffee and 'shore' biscuits. He now wore a buttoned-up white jacket and had combed his hair. He was not very talkative but this was hardly surprising as we had probably interrupted his afternoon nap. We did not realize this at the time.

The main cabin in which we were refreshing ourselves was typical of a bygone age: the 1860's. The old ship's saloon was the full width of the deck-house and, in addition to the settees and the two long, narrow mahogany tables seating eight or ten persons each, there were two serving buffets, fitted with gilt framed mirrors, drawers and cupboards. One was built against the forward bulkhead on the port side and the other aft on the starboard side. I think the material was mahogany with walnut panels. The polished panelling of the saloon reached upwards to the lower sills of the windows on both sides but above this it was enamelled white but the rest of the panelling was polished from deck to deckhead.

Over the centre of each table were polished mahogany racks suspended from rigid, decorative brass pillars. These racks held drinking glasses, a water carafe and condiments in shaped fiddles.

Over the middle of the room was a large flat-topped skylight of oblong shape and fitted with side windows or lights. Daylight in the main cabin was admitted by a number of square ports or windows along each side. They could be opened or closed in similar fashion to that of a railway carriage door windows but they were not fitted with lifting straps. In bad weather they were protected on the outside by removable weather-boards with fixed circular ports in the centres.

The deck-head and the interior of the skylight were white enamelled. There was a fair amount of period fancy-work here. The beam knees were adorned with carved figures while the iron ventilator grilles over the stateroom bulkheads were formed in a lace-like pattern. This whole deck-house had originally contained the first class dining saloon fitted with eight tables and bench-seating in *Lancing*'s days as a passenger liner.

The Master's cabin with its big brass bed was situated on the forepart of the saloon on the starboard side with entry through a doorway in the forward alleyway. At the after end of the saloon, cabins formed a narrow alleyway, offset slightly to starboard of the centreline, the starboard cabin being in use as a passenger cabin though it was actually the room of the Second Mate. A doorway at the after end of this short alleyway led to the main deck, facing the poop bulkhead.

The coffee and all the biscuits having been polished off, we set out on a tour of inspection of the vessel. We paused first at the galley, situated in the after part of the midship deck-house and I met the 'Doctor' who presided over it. He was a large, clean-shaven, broad man with a protruding stomach and an expression of deep thought on his heavy features. Aged about 40, he was a kind man and, as I found out later, an excellent cook, so different from the 'Spoilers of the Deep' to whom I was later to fall victim in practically every vessel I sailed in under the British flag. His pea soup, made with whole peas, was a delicious dream, never to be equalled since!

The galley was entered by a doorway set to starboard of the centreline and the interior was absolutely spotless. I liked the warmth of it and the smell and sound of liquors simmering gently in the pots on the big range against the forward bulk-head. A circular port on either side admitted light and air and an iron skylight overhead ventilated the space. The light from the doorway was reflected from the well-scrubbed red and yellow tiles of the deck. The cook showed us some of the beautiful little stabbing knives of Finnish pattern that he had made and we watched while he poured molten lead into a paper mould round the base of a knife handle. This was his profitable hobby.

Our next call was the fo'c'sle, taking up most of the space in the forward deck-house, where we met the permanent members of the crew who were 'working-by' the ship. They numbered about five and all were Scandinavians aged about 17 to 20. They had ratings of ordinary seamen and deck boys, and possessed the physique of strong men of 30. They were very friendly.

A couple of the hands were putting on their shore clothes preparatory to sampling the delights of a Govan Saturday afternoon. The others were undressing while sitting in their bunks. These latter would sleep the rest of the day away so as to be fit and solvent for an evening ashore with the women in the pubs, or perhaps a visit to the pictures or a music hall with a shipmate.

These young men, who all looked so clean, happy and contented in anticipation of a week-end of freedom with money in their pockets, aroused my envy and I thought then that it would not be long before I was as they were! All had a good command of English but were sometimes puzzled by the school-boy slang which passed between Alan and I. They then would immediately ask for a translation.

The midship deck-house which contained the galley and donkey-room was constructed of iron and was part of the fiddley in her days as a steamer but the fo'c'sle deck-house was constructed of panelled wood and was actually an extension of the saloon deck-house which extended the full length of the ship except for the narrow athwartship alleyway at the poop break.

The interior layout was simple and spartan. The space contained 20 wooden bunks, upper and lowers and all joined together. There were six against the side, two against the after bulkhead athwartships and two more projecting from this on one side of a short centreline partition, and this arrangement was duplicated on the opposite side. A plain, pine table built round two wooden pillars occupied the centre, with a skylight over, and was flanked by wooden bench seats. A sheet iron circular bogey stove, now glowing cherry-red, was situated between the port and starboard doorways in the fore part. Seachests were ranged alongside all the lower bunks, two to the length of a bunk. The ports, which admitted light and air, were small and circular set in oblong portboxes which formed a recess with a flat shelf above and below each port. A large square port or window fitted with sliding louvres opened into the two top athwartship bunks, for this narrow section of the fo'c'sle was originally the second class dining saloon. All bunks were painted dark teak, the wood lining of the house and the deck-head glossy white, while the bunkboards were scarred with the carved names of former occupants.

Leaving the warm and comfortable fo'c'sle we explored the open and enclosed spaces under the fo'c'sle-head. The foremast pierced the two decks here close to the fore part of the fo'c'sle deck-house which extended into this space. On the starboard side of the mast stood a 10-gallon water cask with a hinged half-lid and a brass hasp and staple for a padlock. This was the crew's drinking water so we tasted it, using the tin dipper inside.

Next we had to sharpen our clasp knives on the grindstone in the carpenter's shop. This had a saddle and pedals like a bicycle and a can of water on a gallows over it. The can had a little tap which regulated the flow of water on to the stone. I was not used to this contraption. My knife suddenly closed on a finger and I was called a silly ass! Of course we had to sample the crew's lavatories, though we had been warned that this was prohibited while a ship was in dry dock, since there were other places on the dockside. I thought that this restriction was plain silly as nobody could stop the rain falling in the dock and anything that we could do wouldn't float *Lancing* anyway!

We explored the empty holds, the 'tween decks and looked down into the stinking dungeons of the empty water ballast tanks. After a casual inspection of the former engineroom we returned to the main deck, our happy spirits now dampened by thoughts of what lay before us.

We were going to climb to the top of one of the masts. We had spoken casually and light-heartedly over many weeks, of 'laying out on the royal yards' the next time *Lancing* was in port. We had great conversational courage while the ship was at sea. But now, she was where we had wanted her to be. Standing on the poop deck and gazing aloft, the mast-heads and royal yards appeared to be moving, close to the sweeping clouds. It was an awful long way up. We refrained from looking at each other and then essayed the projected climb to the royal yard. By unspoken agreement we chose the jigger mast as that was the smallest of the four.

Alan started up the starboard rigging while I, climbing on to and over a lifeboat, crossed to the port shrouds and commenced my climb. It was perfectly easy to one who had climbed many a tall, swaying tree and wriggled out on dipping branches, until I reached the eyes of the lower rigging, there the futtock shrouds faced me stretching out and up to the rim of the top above. I would have to continue my climb now with my back facing the deck of the ship, like a fly on a sloping ceiling.

I knew all about 'lubber holes', which enabled a timid or inexpert seafarer to by-pass the terrors of the futtock shrouds by squeezing through the gap between the mast and the decking of the top, that was all right in the days of Lord Nelson when ships had tops as big as kitchens, but merchant ships of a later era have lubber holes a mere six inches wide. Of course I looked hard for the easy way, as I had read enough Marryat to know that it existed, but, alas, I failed to find it.

Alan's red face looked down on me from the security of the top and his breathless voice invited me to join him. This I simply had to do, or he would relate my shame to the whole classroom on Monday morning. Driven by a kind of desperation and a suicidal pride in my ability to succeed whatever the consequences and hanging on with grips of steel which should have squeezed the tar preservative out of the rope ratlines which I was foolish and ignorant enough to hold on to, I struggled out and up until short of breath, trembling and sweating I arrived, weak of knees, in the top.

We stayed on this platform a long time, admiring the view and hoping that people in passing tramcars on their way to the excitement of a football match, would see us and be dumbstruck in their admiration for our daring and skill. I felt like a successful acrobat now that my knees were again solid and I could see that Alan felt the same, though I knew that he had been aloft just this far, with one of the experienced seamen, on a previous visit to the ship.

After a decent interval we held a conference and decided to carry on with our climb to the royal yard, the next stage of which would be a visit to the topsail yards, a mere 16 feet or so above us. Up we started and I immediately noticed a difference. This rigging was loose, compared to the lower rigging which was firm and steady, and had a wide span between the shrouds. The topmast rigging, which I was now climbing, was equipped with wooden battens like the lower rigging but the three shrouds swayed and twisted with my movements. The more often I looked up then down, the less I liked the view.

On the starboard side, the yards were close to the rigging and gave an enveloping sense of security by their nearness, but on my side the yards were a long way away and I seemed to be surrounded by nothing more tangible than atmosphere, except for the swaying shrouds to which I clung.

I looked down at the shrinking, narrowing deck of the ship

and further still, to the bottom of the drydock, and my stomach seemed to shrivel to the size of a pea. Peering upwards towards the eyes of the rigging I thought, what if the wires slipped down the mast because of my weight? Or, if they were in bad condition and should break away altogether? I would go sailing out into space!

As I slowly passed, Alan was standing on the upper topsail yard, gripping the heavy halliard and looking like Amundsen at the Pole. The yard was down on the cap of course but I had to continue upwards. The yards on my side were too far away for me to chance a one-arm swing over the void to them, not this early in my career anyway. I hated to have to keep going up and wondered vaguely what I should do when I reached the cross-trees, now only a foot or so above me. There did not appear to be anything substantial to stand on up there.

But salvation was at hand! A few drops of rain splashed over me and Alan called that he was going down. That was good enough for me. I started down thankfully as the rain increased. The futtock shrouds were a stiffer proposition to negotiate downwards I found, as one could not see where to place one's feet.

It was a wonderful feeling to stand on the firm main deck again and find myself level with the rest of humanity, to feel the muscles relaxing and the strain and tensions easing away, to stretch my cramped fingers straight again, to feel secure. And to know now that I had achieved something, something that was the beginning of a preparation for things to come.

We were soaking wet so we bolted into the warm galley where the Doctor dried our jackets and caps. In the gathering dusk we left the ship, a black, exciting shape, looming and glistening wetly against the smoke-shrouded tenement dwellings and brightly gas-lit shops. As our tram passed the dockyard in which she lay, the yellow lamplight from her ports and doorways, faintly glowing, seemed to me to promise adventure and the first sight of faraway places.

Her dimming shape passed abruptly from view but, from the top platform at the rear of the tramcar, her lower masts and yards soaring towards the wet darkness above could be distinguished as they changed shape and form, played with by light and shadow from the shops and street lamps, until they were but an illuminated memory.

CHAPTER TWO

Months of Waiting . . .

After the visit to the ship we returned to my home, which was the nearest, and Alan asked my opinion of our inspection. I told him that I thought the sailors' teeth were the whitest I had ever seen. This sent him off into gales of laughter whenever he thought of it afterwards and for months he would insist on relating my remark to whomever might be interested, especially if I were present. Later, his sister, Karen, put a stop to it by informing him that I had noticed something which had escaped *his* observation!

I visited the ship many times while she remained in Glasgow, but only once with Alan. He was learning to play the fiddle and had to stay at home on more evenings than I. He could scrape out an aria from *Cavalleria Rusticana* without looking at the music, but it was the only tune I ever heard him play. I think it must have been his party piece.

My visits to the ship ceased when she was moved down river to Ardrossan, Ayrshire. I did not have enough pocket-money or the time necessary to make the journey, so, my main interest in life having departed, I was thrown back to other interests, one of which was nocturnal wanderings.

I loved to roam the streets of the city during the forbidden hours, after I was supposed to be safely in bed. I like the night, its freshness and quietness. In town or country I love to wander around after dark. In the cities, people pass by every second, common people, uncommon people and for some unexplained reason, interesting people. Every hour in Glasgow, on some street corner or back alley, something interesting was happening.

I saw much that I would probably have had to wait years to see, had I not been rebellious. I observed a lot before I reached the age of 16. Fights *en masse*, assignations, accidents, a runaway horse in the centre of the city, open-air, free movies outside the tramway offices and a theatre audience, after a show on a wet night, all trying to get aboard one tram. That was funny. I saw a man with a slashed face lying outside a picture-house and being kicked by two women and a man. While it was still daylight, I saw an elderly clergyman leave a licensed restaurant blind drunk while his two companions of the cloth departed hurriedly from the scene. The drunk sank gently to the pavement.

When it was too cold or wet to make a clandestine exit from my home I usually retired to my attic bedroom at the appointed hour and, donning pyjamas, stood on the foot-rail of the bed with my head out of the skylight watching the stars, the cloud effects and the rain or snow. When I did this I was invariably unhappy and my gaze was usually directed towards the west, where lay the sea.

Sometimes I would wander up to the canal and explore the dark banks, on more than one occasion disturbing the degenerates who haunted the shadows. I was not afraid of them for I could accelerate like a deer and throw a fairly accurate stone. I usually chose moonless nights for my jaunts into the city and bright, moonlit evenings to explore the gloomy and dark places which I already knew well by day.

Alan Blanner informed me one day that, purely as an experience, he was to make a short summer voyage in *Lancing*! My guts twisted with envy. He duly departed; the summer holidays came and went and I returned to school to idle my time away for a further year.

When Alan returned from his voyage in the ship I expected to hear tales of the life he had led and of the adventures which he had surely experienced. I was surprised and shocked to find that he had very little to describe. He had berthed in the double cabin occupied by the Second Mate, had several wrestling matches with the latter who 'was very strong'. He ate in the saloon with the Captain, who had taught him a card game called, 'Skat'! He had also been aloft in a gale of wind and helped to furl the sails. He had helped to load the cargo and had taken some photos of the main deck during heavy weather. Oh yes, the cook had made him a present of a Finnish knife. As he had already two such knives I could not see the value of a third.

The remainder of his report consisted of the good times he

had enjoyed while the ship was loading. Not aboard the ship of course, but in the homes of the shipping people of Cape Chat and Matane in Quebec Province. He had had plenty of social contacts and bored me with the names and social standing of persons to whom even the Captain had to be polite.

Hurricanes—men overboard—falls from aloft—lost sails—boats stoved—collision—fog—fires—sharks—whales? No, nothing like that, but he had received a letter recently from a French-Canadian girl who was a lovely dancer and was 'A bit gone on me, I think. She's a Lulu too!' I pitied him. Poor Alan, the opportunity of a lifetime, and he had been a passenger!

The weary weeks and months dragged on, enlivened only by my visits to the docks. Alan obtained a pass and we visited a big steamer named *Kursk*. She was a Russian ship and Alan knew one of her engineer officers. Since they both spoke Danish while we sat in the officer's cabin, I assumed that she had been taken over during the Revolution and sold to the Scandinavians. Or perhaps she was in the hands of neutrals while a decision was pending. I noticed two revolvers in a small, glass-fronted case fixed to the bulkhead in the officer's bunk. They had the appearance of standard fittings. Unlike most weapons they were not plated or blued.

Some days, I did not bother to attend the last periods of school hours, and, together with kindred spirits, preferred going to the pictures or The Broomielaw, to listening to the big drone of our French master's voice.

Then I had two more months of 'happy, care-free school-days' and nothing had been said or done about my future that I could see, so one afternoon when Alan and I were in the outer office of the Consulate I asked Mr Blanner about the prospects of my sailing in *Lancing*. He replied that if my parents were agreeable, he thought that it could be arranged. After questions about my age and the dates of the school holidays, he left us and returned to his room.

I was radiant. Sure now that the gates of freedom were about to swing abruptly open. Nothing could stop me now, I thought. Mr Blanner had said 'yes'. But he had not said 'yes', he had merely said that he thought that it could be arranged. In my ignorance I had construed his reply to suit myself.

Alan and I were jubilant. He shared my joy, even though he

was to remain at school and would not again sail in the ship. The clerk and the typist both wished me luck. They were the only staff in the Consulate, both Glaswegians. He was a tall, thin, cheerful man with a resonant voice and the manner of a jovial commercial traveller. Quick at repartee, full of humour and ready with a wisecrack to suit any occasion. He had a rather prominent nose and his hair receded well back from his forehead. He usually carried a white-handled steel pen behind his left ear when in the office. Used to dealing with seamen of all nationalities he was the 'leg-man' of the Consulate and spent a good deal of time aboard ships and in dock offices.

The typist was a nice young woman with wavy blonde hair, a good figure and she had a *real* smile. She looked after the tea and biscuits, providing occasional apple or orange rarities, not easy to come by during the war. When important visitors were expected she would produce her standard gripe, 'It's high time we had a decent-looking carpet out here. Just look at the state of this one!' She was right of course. The faded, prone rag in front of the fire had a worn patch in the centre through which a seam in the floorboards could be seen. The whole carpet measured about four by three feet.

The Consulate was a dismal little office situated close to Central Station and reached either by an ancient elevator or a climb up a winding stone staircase. It was a typical small shipping office of the last century. The floor space in the outer office was enclosed by a square-cornered U-shaped counter. On entry, to the right was the typist's desk facing the solitary window which gave a view of other windows in the dirty, white-tiled well. Then came the fire-place and carpet and at the back a high, sloping-topped, double desk, wooden filing cabinets, two chairs and a stool. On the left behind the other wing of the counter was the entrance to Mr Blanner's office.

His private office was more richly furnished and a lot cleaner. He had two builder's half-models of sailing ships on the wall, under a long bookcase shelf with glass sliding doors, facing his large desk. His fire-place was behind him with a big, thick rug in front of it and brightly polished brass poker, tongs and shovel. Even though the outer office required redecorating and cleaning, to me it was redolent of romance and stormy adventure.

I could not get home fast enough on my bicycle to shout the

great news throughout the house, but the fact that I was to sail away in *Lancing* shortly was not received with the wild enthusiasm which I considered it merited. Everyone took it calmly. Father asked for details.

Mother asked, 'When?' and 'What will you need in the way of clothing?'

I had all the details, except a vital one, right at my finger-tips. I ticked them all off.

'Oilskins, leather seaboots with wood pegs in the soles instead of nails, a Green River sheath knife, soap and matches!' I had slipped up there, because the fiction still hung around that I did not smoke, being under age. My error was wisely ignored so I carried on.

'A canvas seabag, a thick blue wool sweater, my jerseys, blue overalls not boiler-suits, overall jackets, thick seaboot socks or stockings, my gym shoes . . .' I paused for breath and an amused voice spoke quietly, 'And a barge to tow behind the *Lancing* to carry all that gear!' It was Dr MacColl, my father's assistant. My father chipped in, saying that when I returned home, a fully qualified seaman, I would be able to get a job on the *Fairy Queen* on the Forth and Clyde Canal. This was a long-standing joke of his, produced whenever I spoke of going to sea.

Well, I was happy; contented for days after that and anyone could get me to run an errand or help with some household chore, without having to say in exasperation, 'For heaven's sake put that book down and . . .!' From then on I haunted the Consulate in my avid desire to sail away to freedom.

The days went sliding slowly by as winter drifted past and the bite went out of the wind and the rain. Spring was in the air as I made my rounds, saying good-bye to my three or four girl friends. I had subsequently to perform this small ceremony twice more with the same girls, since I did not know the date, or even the month, when I would finally depart. But of course I had to let them know in good time so that they would have leisure and opportunity to grieve for me!

My mother laid aside her embroidery and became busy, sewing and patching my old clothes and having me try some on to see if they still fitted. Boots and shoes were sent to the cobblers, if they were judged worth repair, while torn shirts were neatly patched. The number of socks and stockings, which were beautifully darned and rolled into small balls, grew. I had stressed the need for old clothes in which to work when sailing in a windjammer, but to my secret dismay it began to appear as if all I would have to wear would be old clothes—and nothing else!

I did not realize until some months later that my parents must have been fully aware of, and indeed may have been a party to, the arrangements made for my first voyage to sea. I never discovered for I never questioned, but at the time I was under the impression that I had made all the arrangements to launch myself on an unsuspecting world.

Later, when I had compared the outfit which I was given to use aboard *Lancing*, with the full and lavish rig out which I received when I began my apprenticeship in earnest, I came to the conclusion that my first voyage was a trial trip, agreed to in the hope that I would have the overload of 'romantic nonsense' knocked out of me by the hardest and roughest kind of seafaring still surviving.

One of my final social calls was Mr Grant, the Principal of a firm of stationers in Renfield Street, Glasgow. Seeing him in the shop I informed him of my future destination. Our family obtained all our school stationery from the store where we had an account. I liked Mr Grant. He was a small, frail man with a very gentle manner, usually dressed in grey. He was a widower and also was very short-sighted, wearing spectacles with lenses as thick as binoculars. He once told me that my names were very suitable for a title, and how right he was!

Starting with the title bestowed on me by our domestic staff, 'That Devil', I think I have been the recipient, since then, of every kind of name, thought up on the spur of the moment or, after long cogitation, by men and women of divers nationalities throughout the world.

Mr Grant was interested to hear that I was starting my sea career in a sailing ship and recalled the names of some famous vessels. Leaving me to browse around for a while he returned with four pocket-sized volumes of classical tales of the sea which he gave me. One was a Conrad, as I remember. As I was leaving he wished me good fortune and safe voyaging and advised me to keep a diary and my eyes wide open since I would be certain to have experiences which I might wish to write about in later life.

CHAPTER THREE

. . . *Till I Join Her at Last*

The month of June had come and I had said my farewells to my friends at school and to the few masters that I favoured. I have no distinct recollection of leaving the building, instead I just seemed to disappear into thin air, and unlike many boys in similar circumstances, I never paid a return visit. I had seen some of these re-visiting 'old boys' and they had all appeared to be too full of their own importance and to wish us to add to their self-glorification. As for me, why go back except to gloat over the place I abhorred and from which I was free? I had better things to do than hob-nob with my former gaolers.

The family were preparing to depart for a holiday some-where and I began to have apprehensions. I had not as yet received any concrete instructions regarding a berth or a sailing date. I still haunted the Consulate but never seemed to be able to catch Mr Blanner in the outer office. He was always busy and if he appeared before us it was only to ask a question of the staff before nodding to me and disappearing into his private office again just as I was about to open my mouth.

Finally, one day I did speak to him, with the help of the typist who had taken pity on my worries and informed her chief that I would like an interview. I was not ushered into the sanctum. Mr Blanner came into the main office and informed me that he could not help me any further. If I wanted to sail in *Lancing*, I must ask the Captain myself!

I was shaken to the core at this surprising news. He must have seen the consternation reflected in my face for he laughed and waved his papers towards the door. 'Captain Pedersen has just left here. He is going back aboard the ship and if you hurry, you might just catch him before the train leaves!'

With a hasty farewell over my shoulder, I shot through the

doorway, down the stone stairs and made for Central Station
at top speed, heedless of traffic. I knew that the train for
Ardrossan usually departed from platforms 12 or 13 and I
weaved through the crowds of people as though I were playing
Rugby and had the ball.

Sighting the captain standing beside a kiosk I rushed up to
him, saying breathlessly, 'Captain, Mr Blanner told me to ask
you if I could sail in *Lancing*, Sir?' He was a big, burly man, over
six feet in height with tanned features and a flowing black
moustache. He wore a grey overcoat and a black trilby hat.
Standing close in front of him I was a mere shrimp of five feet.

He looked down at me for a full minute, as though he were
examining his boots, then removing the big straight-stemmed
pipe from his mouth, cleared his throat and spoke in abrupt
official tones.

'As a passenger?' With a flash of insight I knew that if I said
yes, I would never sail in the ship. I quickly answered, 'No,
sir, I want to be a sailor!'

He nodded without speaking, returned the pipe to his mouth,
sucked, and expelled a cloud of thick, stinking smoke which
eddied around my head, then told me to obtain my father's
permission and join the ship on the following Saturday in
Androssan. That would give me a day or two, he said, to shake
down aboard and get used to things before the ship put to sea!

During the following week, our home resounded with
questions and answers and they were all concerned with my
outfitting for the rigours of the Western Ocean. My mother
casually suggested that I might like to take some of my favourite
eatables along with me. I scorned the idea! What would the
other seamen think of a man who brought his own scones
aboard?

I'm sure that I must have driven my poor mother nearly
frantic during that last week at home. Some of the trouble
arose from the fact that though I had plenty of disconnected
knowledge about ships, none of it stemmed from experience.
But this did not stop me from thinking that I was some kind of
a marine oracle.

The seabag was purchased and delivered and when opened
out on the dining room table, the smell of new canvas and the
shine of brass eyelets was a strange invasion of our home. I

became busy on it at once, and removing it to the kitchen and
stretching it flat on one of the tables, I proceeded to sketch
my name and that of my ship, on one side of the bag.

G. CRAIG

4/M Skib *Lancing*

KRISTIANIA

When inked-in with black, red and green colours and hanging over the kitchen pulleys to dry, the print looked quite
imposing and seemed, to my eyes, to give a firm destination to
my life at last. I had to explain to the servants that the word
'skib' was the Norwegian designation of 'ship' and the '4/M'
simply meant that the vessel had four masts.

There was plenty of excitement when I donned a pair of my
new overalls and paraded in front of the family. I could see
that my mother did not like to see me in the rig of a 'common
seaman' and though I had heard the words many times from
her lips in the past, this time she was non-committal. However,
the three suits would have to be altered. The legs of the
trousers and the sleeves of the jackets were too long and
required shortening. This she proceeded to do.

By about Wednesday or Thursday the bag was finally packed
and despite my remonstrances, my pyjamas were included. I
had to give in for the sake of peace but I stood firm on the
matter of my dressing-gown. Pyjamas could be hidden but not
that other thing, and I was not going to be made to look
ridiculous aboard my first ship. No seaman ever wore pyjamas.
I knew! And as for a dressing-gown, never! I was prepared for
a tough life, and tough it was going to be, and that was that!
The dressing-gown remained at home and I concealed the
pyjamas later.

The seabag was too heavy for me to carry, so a horse cab was
ordered and I proceeded alone in it to Central Station where
I purchased a third single to Ardrossan and sent the bag ahead
as luggage in advance. I would follow on the Saturday. I had
some trouble explaining to the clerk that my destination was
Ardrossan in Ayrshire and not Lancing in Sussex, as he
appeared to think from an inspection of the decorative lettering
on the canvas.

I happened to be present in the Consulate the following
afternoon when a crowd of seamen were being engaged for the

forthcoming voyage. They were a mixture of races and nationalities. Danes, Norwegians and Swedes. There were not enough of them to make up a full crew so the remainder were being recruited in Greenock, Liverpool and Ardrossan, and sent to the ship direct.

The men, foregathered in front of the office counter, looked like seamen and appeared to me to be a rough but able crowd, such as I had observed times without number on my excursions around Glasgow docks. They wore no collars or ties, but over a blue jersey or striped flannel shirt was a large coloured hand-kerchief worn as a scarf. None owned an overcoat, or ever had done so. Their suits were of shoddy material and, judging by the creases, appeared to have been slept in recently, that is, the few complete suits visible.

Most of the men wore odd garments, a jacket of one colour and material and trousers of another, while a couple were tailored above the waist and overalled below. Nearly all wore cloth caps of various patterns and they favoured boots and shoes of weird and wonderful designs and shapes, very foreign in appearance. I noticed that their hands were large, hairy and the palms calloused and thickened while the hands at rest had fingers bent inwards. Some fingers were deformed by injury while the backs of most hands bore a tattoo of a mariner's compass, or other crude design. All spoke across the counter in English but conversed with each other in Scandanavian languages.

Mr Blanner was present when the question of a bo'sun was raised by the clerk. A slight, bent, nondescript Dane, in need of a shave with a flowing sandy moustache and hair to match, blue eyes and the usual weather-beaten complexion, who had on his head a badgeless, black uniform cap having rucked ribbon edging around the visor, and was clothed in a black double-breasted pilot jacket, spoke up quickly, too quickly I thought, 'I'll take the bosun's job!'

I was struck by the cool cheek of the man, to claim a post which had not been offered yet, without prior consultation with the ship's Master, who was not present at this preliminary engagement session.

The shipping clerk spoke sharply to him, 'The ship is not carrying a bo'sun on this voyage.'

Mr Blanner intervened, 'Put him down as carpenter. He is paying-off in Canada and will need a little extra money.' Turning to the claimant, he asked. 'Carpenter's berth suit you? You can manage it?'

The reply delivered in an American accent was satisfactory and the job of donkeyman was next allocated to a dark, saturnine individual.

Various men were told in what capacity they would serve, until there was only me left. The clerk thought that I was to be a passenger but I soon put that idea out of his head.

'I'm a deck boy and I'm going in the fo'c'sle with the rest of the men,' I announced.

Mr Blanner nodded, 'Yes, that's right.' I received some slightly surprised glances from the assembled seamen, for as far as they could see, I was on the wrong side of the counter.

As I left the office, the seamen were still trying to obtain an advance on their prospective earnings before joining the ship. But I had heard that they would be unlucky, as all they would get would be a railway ticket to Ardrossan, and the clerk would see them all on to the train and the train out of the station, before he left them. Their advance of money would be in the form of an advance note, cashable where convenient, after they had actually signed on the ship.

During the next two days my greatest fear was that my mother would want to travel to Ardrossan with me. I had expressed my fears to my sisters with the object in view that they might be able to dissuade my mother from such a drastic and fatal expedition. The roundabout plan must have been effective for very sensibly, my parents asked the assistant, Dr MacColl, to travel to Ardrossan with me and purchase some needful sea-gear on the spot, such as oilskins, seaboots, bedding and a knife.

Saturday dawned, but I have only the dimmest recollections of leaving home. The good-byes and the tears of my mother, the two pound notes pressed into my hand by my father, the 'Good luck, Master Gavin' of the servants and the smiles and happy waves of my sisters grouped around the garden gate as the taxi drove away. My mind was already installed aboard the ship.

Long before the train arrived at Ardrossan, my head was protruding from the carriage window and I was eager to announce to Dr MacColl, 'There she is, that's her!'

We were driven from the station in a horse cab to Eglington Dock, where *Lancing* lay alongside, almost ready for sea. We found ourselves within ten minutes, facing the dock entrance, a line of inverted U-shaped railings and a swinging wicket-gate beside railway metals extending into the dock area. Ahead of us was the stern of the ship and, etched against the sky, her lofty masts, 200 feet from keelson to truck!

Dr MacColl accompanied me on a brief tour of the vessel after which we sallied ashore to buy some gear at Sinclair's in Princes Street. This was a seamen's outfitters. It was not a large shop, though it had two, many-paned windows, and was approached by three or four wooden steps at the entrance. The interior was dim but colourful. A short wooden counter was placed to the right of the doorway and another at right angles to it, near the back of the shop, on the left. The rest of the furniture consisted of shelves heaped with folded overalls, jackets, jerseys, flannel shirts and woollen underwear.

There were cartons of soap bars and bars without cartons, packets of safety matches; working boots, shoes, belts, braces, seaboots suspended from the shelves by string, and piles of rough blankets. The stock overflowed on to the floor. Nests of galvanized iron buckets, rubber seaboots for steamer seamen, piles of folded oilskin coats, trousers and jackets, and small barrels and cases as yet unopened.

More stock was suspended from hooks in the wooden ceiling. Enamelled tin cups threaded together by string through the handles, jugs, oilskin coats on hangers, guitars, mandolines, a couple of fiddles, while some cheap, ready-made suits on hangers occupied a place of honour facing the doorway. In one corner near the left-hand window were two piles of straw-filled mattresses, or 'donkeys'-breakfasts', rolled and tied in the middle with string. A grimy old glass show-case on the small counter near the doorway, supported a piano-accordion, while inside the case were Green River sheath knives, sewing palms, sail needles, mouth-organs, and highly polished Ingersoll watches.

As we advanced into the gloom of the interior a little, stout, grey-haired man wearing a black alpaca jacket and a black

velvet pillbox cap embroidered with gold threadwork came
forward to meet us, smiling. With my assistance and the advice
and promptings of the stout gentleman, I was fitted out with a
long oilskin coat, sou'wester, knife, sheath and belt, seaboot
socks and real leather seaboots of surprisingly good quality
which lasted me a very long time, until my feet grew out of
them, three or four blankets, a mattress and a pillow.

I think that this completed the purchases and the proprietor
promised to have the lot delivered to the ship before six o'clock.
I would not wait for this and insisted on taking some of my
sea-gear aboard forthwith. The bedding could follow later. So,
clutching the heavy brown paper parcel to my chest we
returned to the ship and I deposited the lot in my bunk. I have
only a hazy recollection of saying good-bye to Dr MacColl on the
station platform, as the final link with my home was severed.

On that first lonely evening I hastened to shift into my new,
stiff overall pants, which seemed to smell of linoleum, sheath
knife and belt and grey flannel working shirt. I recollect refus-
ing an invitation to go ashore to the Eglington Arms for I was
very happy to be left alone in a practically deserted ship.

I scampered aloft on at least three of her four masts, having
long ago conquered my fear of the bare heights and having, on
my third visit to the ship, reached the jigger royal yard. But it
was not until I had been aloft several times, that I had ventured
out to the royal yard-arm. I had been out on the other yards,
where the upper topsail and upper t'gallant were close together
and I could walk on each of the lower yards, but there seemed
to be an awful lot of empty space under the royal yards and
moving my feet along a thin wire footrope about 150 feet above
the deck, was a matter for some mature consideration—until
the day came when I did it. After that I was confident and sure.

I had not yet had a meal but I had been summoned aft by
the Steward who had received a wooden case addressed to me.
Red lettered labels were plastered over it announcing FRAGILE—
WITH CARE. It was unopened but he informed me that it
probably contained food which he would issue to me, as and
when I required it.

I did not like the idea of that at all. I have never approved
of other people controlling my property but I thanked the
Steward for his advice, which included the observation that the

other foremast hands would soon make short work of my gift. Picking up the heavy case I staggered off, forward, and deposited it on the fo'c'sle table where I proceeded to open it with my new sheath knife.

It consisted for the most part of boiled sweets in glass jars, Scotch shortbread, tins of biscuits and a chocolate-iced cake with a thick cream filling. I ate most of the cake there and then. Packing the shelves of the portbox with some of this bonanza and leaving a jar of sweets handy to my pillow, I stowed the remainder in the seachest which I had appropriated and half-filled with my gear.

I had, in my ignorance, taken over 'a bunk with a view' situated on the starboard side, opposite the table. It was a top bunk fitted with a port and was in the second tier. Surprisingly, I was permitted to retain possession throughout the voyage. Why the able seamen did not throw me out and consign me to one of the dark lower bunks I do not know. I can only surmise that, as the ship was bound on a cold Atlantic voyage and would not pass through the tropics, the senior seamen preferred the lower and warmer bunks, rather than cope with a leaking port and a damp mattress. As it turned out, my port leaked only slightly and then only from a direct blow of a boarding sea.

The day had been a long and tiring one and I think it must have been about nine o'clock when I turned in. I chose to place my pillow at the wrong end of the bunk, the after end. I did this because the port was there and I liked to look out through the fore rigging. It is customary for the seamen to lie with their heads forward. I imagine that this arrangement arose because of the curved sheer of ships.

There was nobody in the fo'c'sle, though I knew that the Steward and the Chief Mate were aboard. I had seen the latter come out on deck and look aloft at me swinging in the rigging. He must have been satisfied at my ability to move around up there, for he had retired without calling me down, and it was still daylight. In my room at home, I would have read myself sleepy with a 'tuppenny blood' or a Western magazine, but not here. From the moment that I joined this ship I had abandoned all such forms of literature and years were to pass before I looked at them again.

The scent of straw was strong in my nostrils, the pillow was hard and prickly and the mattress creaked and rustled on the hard boards as I turned from side to side. My eyes were heavy with encroaching sleep when the loud sound of footsteps on the iron deck outside brought my head round and my eyes towards the doorways.

A big man followed by another stumbled into the gloom of the fo'c'sle. The first man swore in Norwegian and fumbled for matches while the other groped around then placed two bottles on the table. The small paraffin lamp was lit and the lamp glass replaced before they noticed me.

The big fellow smiled and roared loudly, 'Yesus, Yack, why you no light d'lamp?'

The other asked me if I would like a drink. Thinking of lemonade I was about to say yes, when the big seaman spoke. 'This be good strong Scottish beer, Yack.'

I'm afraid I replied a trifle primly, 'No thanks, I don't touch liquor.'

They both grinned broadly, and the smaller of the two laughed and said, 'You don' touch likker, eh boy? What about wimmen? You like girls?'

The other broke in, 'Naw, he don' lik 'em either!' He grinned broadly when I hastened to correct him.

They produced pint-sized enamelled mugs and questioned me about my amorous experiences while they drank. Of course I lied, manfully. They appeared surprised that I was aged 16, as from my size they had thought that I was only about 14. Fresh arrivals bringing more bottles, brought the inquisition to an end and the talk from then on ignored me and centred on the pubs they had been in, the women they had fancied and could not afford, the ships and steamers they had sailed in previously, *Lancing*'s sailing qualities under different combinations of sail and the effect they had on her steering, the Captain, the Mates, the Cook and the food, until weary with this exciting day, I fell sound asleep in my new, but not strange, surroundings.

CHAPTER FOUR

Signed On

My morning sleep was rudely disturbed by hoarse voices and the thumping of heavy hands on my bunkboard as several calls penetrated to me. 'Come on, Yack, turn out. Coffeeeee!'

Regretfully, I rolled slowly out and, standing on my seachest as I stepped into my pants, I fully expected to see the breakfast laid out ready. My sleepy eyes saw only a large steaming can with an iron wire handle. I was shocked to find that the time was 5.55 a.m., and I remembered then that we would have to work on deck or aloft for two full hours before we would have a hot meal.

I stuffed some biscuits into the pockets of my overall jacket and, swallowing a sip or two of good strong coffee, well sugared, I regretted that the cup was too hot to down the contents in the time available. The thin sound of a small bell aft tinged two double notes and a sailor who happened to be nearest the door dashed quickly out of the fo'c'sle and struck the same number of sounds on the big bell hanging between decorative metal dolphins at the after end of the deck-house.

We, about eight men and youths, garbed in a variety of old clothes, left the fo'c'sle smartly and moved forward to collect our deck brooms. Then we proceeded aft again and met the Second Mate who was waiting for us outside the galley doorway.

The Second Mate was young, about 25 or so, clean-shaven, sandy-haired, squarely built and muscular, and about five feet eight inches tall. He was possessed of a sense of humour and was not easily provoked. He was a strict and a just man. If we boys did not presume to look upon him with affection, well, he had his job to do and we had ours so we all knew clearly where we stood. He beckoned to me and two others and told us to start our labours by washing down the poop deck.

As we accompanied the officer aft, other seamen were rolling an empty cask along the iron main deck towards the poop deck-house. The main deck on both sides of the house was sheathed with wood, and, with the fo'c'sle-head decking, were the only wood decks in the ship, open to the weather. The poop deck, including the top of the deck-house, was covered with painted canvas as a protection against leaks, probably owing to the age of the vessel.

The cask was set upright near the wheel-house doorway, a tail block was hitched to the mizzen topsail brace and a canvas draw bucket made fast to the rope whip rove off through the block. A man, standing on the mainrail, drew water from the dock and filled the cask. The second mate dashed water over the deck from a bucket filled by one of us from the cask while two of us scrubbed with our deck brooms, using, as instructed, the wrong side of the bristles.

While we scrubbed the decks, the seaman on the draw bucket worked hard to keep the cask filled, when he could have a brief rest, but it was up to us to see that he did not have too much rest, since it was to our advantage that the cask was kept full. The full buckets were heavy when lifted from low down inside the cask, but comparatively light when filled near the top, or so we thought.

I wondered why some of the men had donned oilskin jackets on such a fine, dry day but I was soon to find out. When we had worked our way as far as the jigger mast my broom was given to another and I was told to stand half way up one of the poop ladders and pass the full buckets up to the officer, receiving in return, the empties. In passing the heavy oaken buckets up, my strength and skill were insufficient for the task and each bucket tipped slightly, spilling a little of the contents down on me! After about four buckets I was soaked to the skin.

We washed and scrubbed our way along the iron main deck and finished by scrubbing the fo'c'sle-head, the seats, the steps and the decks of the crew's lavatories and filling the casks inside them, then we put our brooms away.

It was now about seven o'clock on Sunday morning and while some of the others were put to drying and polishing brasswork about the poop, I was given the job of cleaning and polishing the big brass bell on the deck-house. When eight bells were struck aft, we were finished for the day and I made sure that it was I who answered on the big shining instrument!

I quickly changed into dry clothes and abstracted a soggy mass of ruined biscuits from my wet jacket pockets. One of the sailors told me to 'Give a hand to bring the grub along!', which I gladly did. The breakfast consisted of porridge, or 'burgoo' as it is called in all ships. With this we were given powdered cinnamon, in place of sugar or syrup, together with condensed milk made liquid by the addition of water. The cinnamon was new to me but I liked it. Then we had fried bacon with one egg and unlimited coffee. I had carried the half-gallon butter tin filled with coffee and put it on the table but was told, 'Stick it on the bogey, Yack!' So I hurriedly placed it on top of the big sheet-iron stove and hastened to claim my share of the eatables.

The small loaves of bread issued to us as a ration were fresh and warm and of good quality with a nice, thick pale crust, but they did not last very long. With the bread we had lots of jam but not much margarine. The food was plain and well cooked and was highly appreciated after two solid hours on deck, carrying around an empty stomach. I resolved to turn out earlier after this, *if I could*, so as to get my share of the coffee before four bells were struck.

After I had helped to return the empty food 'kits' to the galley the rest of the seamen drifted out on deck and we sat on the main hatch smoking and talking. I did most of the listening. A seaman fetched a bucket in which clothes were steeping. He gave the shirts and underwear a quick rinse through and laid them on a newspaper spread on the deck while he went aft to the galley to beg a bucketful of hot, fresh water. Having obtained this prize he sat on a lower step of the fo'c'sle-head ladder with the bucket between his feet and washed the clothing slowly and methodically, soaping small sections of a garment and rubbing them between his knuckles.

I watched another sailor wash his overall pants, laying them on the iron deck, well soaped, and scrubbing them with a hand scrubber. When he had given them a final rinse he folded them equally and placed the loop behind a spare belaying pin on the mainrail. Then he grasped the two parts and twisted them together, his biceps swelling and straining as the water streamed down and the garment began to look like a horizontal rope. When he untwisted the pants and shook them I saw that now they were merely damp.

The subjects of conversation of my shipmates on the main-hatch ranged far and wide. I strained my ears eagerly to the parts which were related in English and I learned a good deal about the brothels in Callio, Santos, Nouméa and the Boca in Buenos Aires, together with the current charges in these exciting establishments.

My parents had not seen fit to impart the 'facts of life' to me as they probably surmised that I would at once try to fit the facts to my personal life. But there was little need for a sex lecture as I had long ago learned the basic elements from the conversations of older boys at school, observing courting couples in the heather, on golf courses and the quieter beaches of holiday resorts—and from the books in my father's library!

Reading these books, or parts of them, enlightened me on some aspects of sexual behaviour but there was a great deal which I did not understand and some parts which I could not bring myself to believe to be true! The unbelievable deformities or elephantiasis illustrated by photographs in a volume on tropical diseases rendered me speechless—for a day or so! The grounding in the Latin language which had been thumped into me was useful here. Many of these medical books contained coloured sectional illustrations, especially dealing with surgery, and I imagine that my early ability to read blueprints started there. But the horrors depicted had their share in convincing me that membership of the medical profession was not for me!

Noon found us congregated round the fo'c'sle table for the share out of the midday meal. Someone had again told me, 'Get busy, Yack, an' bring the scran from the galley!' Another had admonished, 'An' hurry up, we don' want a cold bloody dinner!'

I, of course, did what my seniors told me to do. I attended outside the galley doorway and a tin kit or kid containing food was handed to me over the closed lower-half of the door. I duly thumped down the container on the scrubbed table and dived into my seachest for plate and 'tools' as others arrived with the other dishes.

Our meal was composed of vegetable soup, stewed beef with greens, potatoes and gravy, and a concoction called 'fruit-grut'. This was a grey, jelly-like shimmering mass with berries in it. I did not care for it, mainly because of its appearance, but when I was hungry I ate it. I also learned to eat, and usually to enjoy, *fiskeballas* (my spelling is phonetic: they were fish cakes), *lobscouse* (stew), *baccalow* (salt cod or stockfish) and various other dishes new to me.

It was a day of sunshine and while the other seamen slept or went ashore, I climbed around on the masts and yards or made my way to the quayside and strolled around, looking at *Lancing* from a distance, for I now had a proprietary interest in her. This 'looking' was performed in a surreptitious manner, with brief swinging glances as my head turned this way and that. I did not want the casual observer to think that the ship was so new to me that she was the object of my veneration, like that a husband not long married has for an attractive wife. I wanted the world to believe when they saw us together that I was used to her.

The day drifted slowly by and when the fo'c'sle lamp was lit I wrote, much against my natural inclinations, a letter home. A one-page epistle, saying that I was all right and the ship would be sailing shortly. 'Give my love to . . . all my fondest love to both of you, your loving son, Gavin.' That was the last direct news that my parents had of me until I was on the way home again. I did not like writing home for I knew that my mother read my letters aloud at the breakfast table! And to all our relatives! And to all her personal friends! So writing home became an exercise which I seldom indulged in.

The following day, after the decks had been washed down, we were employed aloft bending t'gallant sails and royals which had been repaired by the sailmaker. I liked this work, it was interesting, far more so than the job which two of the other seamen were engaged on down in the hold. Supervised by the old Chief Mate they were hardening down the nuts on the ballast tank lids. Their work consisted of going round and round each lid with large spanners attached to lengths of piping screwing down tight the nuts and bolts which secured the lids to the flanges of the tank coamings. All the tanks had been battened down the previous week, but this was an additional precaution to prevent leakage. The job called for strength and reach, so I suppose that was the reason why they were down there and I was up aloft.

When we turned to after dinner I received a sharp reprimand from the Second Mate because I had walked out on deck smoking a cigarette. I had forgotten for the moment that we were not permitted to smoke while working. Neither were we allowed inside the fo'c'sle during our watch on deck. The rule was, 'Watch on deck—Stop on deck'.

About four o'clock the remainder of the crew joined the ship, the men from Glasgow whom I had already seen, one or two from Greenock or Port Glasgow and a fairly mixed bag from Liverpool, numbering about seven, three of whom proved to be first class seamen who invariably chose to sail in square-rigged ships and schooners. Two of the others were quite young men who had served only in steamers but they quickly became used to the duties of seamen in a sailing ship.

The remaining two men of this lot were not a damn bit of use. One of them was a scruffy, dirty, religious maniac whose main preoccupation when off watch was to sit in his bunk and read the Bible *aloud*, until this habit was stopped by dire threats. Threats also had to be used to induce him to wash! He was quickly renamed, 'Jesuschrist'.

The other man was an ex-apprentice who had served his time in steamers out of the Port of London. He was a loud-mouthed 'blowhard', aged about 22. A boy who had gone to seed. He affected a tough attitude and a spurious cockney accent. Every second or third word he uttered was a needless oath. To hear him talk, one was given the impression that an average of three or four girls a week had been used and tossed aside and that when it came to drinking, he was a two-bottle man! He was known as 'Ed' and was neither competent nor reliable but he had been engaged as an able seaman.

Of the three good seamen from Liverpool one was a Dane, I think, aged about 38 with a reddish complexion. I privately thought of him as the 'Farmer' for he looked like one. He was a kindly man, easily amused, who smiled much but laughed rarely. The second was a young Finn, short, plump, pale-faced and aged about 25, very strong and possessed of a mean and nasty disposition. His features were rather good and regular and he had blond hair and very pale blue eyes which somehow reminded me of a fish.

The third man was to me, and, I imagine to others too, a bit of a mystery. His age would be maybe 50. He was respected as an excellent seaman and was strong and active with a clear and rather pale skin and wise, grey eyes. He had thick, curly, black hair and a big, black beard and moustache which he occasionally trimmed with small scissors. The beard used to part in the centre with the force of the wind, giving him a likeness to the German Admiral von Tirpitz. His speech was cultured, rapid and concise. He did not express himself very often, but if he chose to insert himself into a discussion or argument, everyone stopped talking instantly to listen to what he had to say and they generally accepted his opinion. His manner was quietly authoritative and one sensed that he was accustomed to issuing orders. My shipmates came to the inevitable conclusion that he had been a shipmaster who had been unlucky.

Looking back at him now, I think that there was more to him than that. He was too intelligent a man to spend the remainder of his life in ships' fo'c'sles, if he had once had command. He had none of the signs of failure. I think he had chosen his way of life, perhaps awaiting circumstances to arrange a pattern which would be beneficial to him. In my mind I named him 'Blackbeard' and now I am grateful to him because he told me a lot about ships, the seas and the weather, in odd moments. But he never attempted to lecture me pontifically, as was the custom in schools.

*   *   *

During the remainder of the afternoon there was a constant movement of men, in and out of the fo'c'sle, emptying seabags, filling seachests, hanging oilskin suits and other sea gear on pegs or handy nails and generally sorting themselves out and finding their place in the ship. Then the Second Mate appeared amongst us and, in the sudden hush caused by his appearance in the doorway, informed all hands in mixed sentences of Norwegian and English that they were required to lay aft in the cabin and sign on the ship!

We all trooped aft and shyly entered the cabin alleyway

47

where we stood in a long loose-packed queue with the boys at the tail end and the seamen holding their caps in their hands or stuffing them into their hip pockets. Slowly the crocodile edged along, as men pushed past holding their Advance Notes, on their way out on deck again and then to the brief freedom of the streets. I was halted at the door of the officers' messroom and glimpsed the two Mates sitting in facing seats talking and laughing. The line moved again as I and the rest of the boys shuffled towards the cabin doorway until it was possible to glimpse the familiar interior of the saloon.

The starboard table was in use as a counter on which to sign the Contract, or Articles of Agreement. A group of people were sitting on the settee, facing us across the table, the Shipping Master, the representative of the Norwegian Consulate, one other whom I took to be a clerk, or he might have been an Immigration Official, Mrs Pedersen, the wife of the Captain, was seated in a movable armchair at the after part of the room, standing beside her was one of her sons, a boy of about 14 years of age. Captain Pedersen was not seated but moved about the big room, puffing at that awful pipe and watching the ceremony.

I overheard that we were to have two passengers on the voyage, the young son of the Captain was to sail with us and an elderly Scottish stockbroker who had already made one voyage in the ship, for his health. The Captain's dog, a black-and-tan nuisance would also voyage with us, at least part of the way!

I remember signing my name with a scratching pen dipped into an ink bottle and being asked if I desired an Advance Note or wished to leave an allotment to dependent relatives. I had no need for either since I still had a pound left of the money given to me by my father. I received a nice smile and a few encouraging words from Mrs Pedersen who I thought was very attractive. I believe she was Scottish before her marriage. Then I was out on deck again where work had finished for the day.

Before the mast the vessel carried a carpenter, sailmaker, donkeyman, bo'sun, bo'sun's mate, eleven able seamen, three ordinary seamen and four deck boys: 23 hands.

In the afterguard, there were the Master and two mates, one steward, one cook and two passengers. I was surprised to see on the crew list later that I am described as *letmatros* or ordinary seaman, as were other deck boys, and that a cabin boy was listed. This latter was probably one of the deck boys who lived with us in the fo'c'sle and was required to scrub out the cabins occasionally. He must have been in the other watch. I do not remember any cabin boy. I do know that my Discharge Book describes me as *dekksgutt* or deck boy.

As I recollect, two of the regular hands had been promoted from ordinary to able seamen and two Scottish young men had been given their jobs. These lads were two brothers, aged about 18 or 19. They were decent young fellows, both quiet and sensible. They sang well in harmony, too.

Back in the fo'c'sle all was talk and explanations. The Scandinavians were explaining to the Britishers the relative values of kroner and ore and pounds, shillings and pence. Lanky, loud-mouthed Ed was out on deck with shaving mirror propped against the t'gallant rail while, with many grimaces, he guided a safety razor through the soapy lather on his stupid, narrow horse-face and repeatedly bawled the information that, 'The —— —— hatches is off, mate!' Meaning that the pubs were now open. Now that they all had money, or the value of it in the form of an Advance Note, their one thought was to get rid of it before the ship sailed in the morning!

Across the fo'c'sle table, the Farmer proposed that, as they were all going ashore to cash their notes, now was the time to have a whip round for the purchase of a musical instrument. This proposal, because it appeared to be a traditional custom in such ships, found general agreement and proportionate amounts were fixed according to the number of petty officers and seamen before the mast. Some of the men, who already had a few shillings, dropped their share on the table while I dived into my seachest and came up with five shillings. But I was told to keep it. None of the seamen would take a boy's money and nothing that I could say or do would induce them to accept my cash. There were a few of us boys in the fo'c'sle and we felt a bit hurt that they would not consider our donations. Secretly, I think we felt that it would have set the seal on our 'belonging' to the regular professional crew of a windjammer. But it appeared to be a custom of the sea and we had to abide by it!

We made our important way up Eglington Street and into Sinclar's shop where my sea gear had been purchased and as various instruments were being given a try out, other members of the ship's crew entered, purchased clothing of one kind or another, and cashed their Advance Notes. Judging by the remarks they made and their gestures, they were charged a fairly stiff rate of interest. When the remainder of the money had been collected by the Farmer, an accordion costing £7 10s was purchased and the members of the committee moved across the street to the Eglinton Arms.

I had been invited to go with them but my Presbyterian upbringing had led me to believe that there was something demonic lurking in every public house and, because I did not like the smell of beer and had not yet worked this fear out of my system, I declined politely and returned aboard with a bag full of cream cakes.

The news that a ship had signed on had brought the women down to the docks and I had to push my way through them in order to reach the wicket gate and the quay. I was even invited to, 'Come oan an hae a short-time wi me, ma wee laddie!' by a grey haired broken-nosed 'shawlie' whose age must have been topping 50! I was amazed that such an elderly woman should even have considered having relations with someone of my age, or should think that I would consent to go to bed with a dustbin like her! What could she see in me that was attractive to her, or vice versa? I had, of course, overlooked the financial side of her proposal. I had always thought, from conversations I had overheard, that 'elderly' women, over 30, were sexless and finished with exciting life, except for dressing up, visiting and talking about their past life and their friends, cooking and sewing.

A policeman was standing outside the level-crossing gates but he only smiled and joked with the women. His duty appeared to be 'disturbance prevention': to see that they did not go inside the dock estate and get aboard the ships, since fighting usually broke out amongst a drunken crew when this happened.

I had not been long aboard when those of the crew who had been ashore in their working gear returned, to clean themselves up, eat their supper and change into their shore-going rig. They brought the accordion with them and Pelle (it was pronounced Pail-la), a young seaman who turned out to be the player with the most extensive repertoire, deposited it in his bunk. Later, it was always kept in a spare lower bunk and could be used by anyone who could play it.

Again, I was left alone in my end of the ship. I finished my supper, played with the ship's cat which I had enticed away from the galley, sucked and blew a few mournful airs on my mouth-organ, returned the kids of left-over food to the galley and looked at the pictures in a bundle of magazines which someone had brought aboard from some Mission in the town.

Then I thought it would be a good idea to go ashore again, maybe to the pictures and have a feed of ice cream which would take the form of a double 'Macallum', and finally a call at some chip shop for two mutton pies, chips and peas to complete the evening. So I changed into my grey suit and instead of a collar and tie I donned a blue jersey which I thought would give me a real sailorlike appearance.

About an hour later I met Pelle and another young seaman named Larvik up the town. They were on a pub-crawl and were taking life easy. I was invited to go with them as they drew abreast of a public house but when I declined the invitation they nodded casually, pushed open the doors and vanished into the smoky, noisy, gas-lit and beer-reeking atmosphere. A couple of years later I was doing the same thing myself in Liverpool, Birkenhead, Avonmouth, Le Havre, Dunkirk, Hamburg, Venice and Rangoon.

Back aboard the ship with a swollen stomach and a restless mind, I was sitting in my bunk with legs dangling over the bunkboard when the big Russian and a small fat man with a flushed, pudgy and brutal face, entered and placed the inevitable bottles on the table with a clinking series of thumps. They were both well away, the fat man more so than the Russian. We all knew the latter's nationality but officially he was classed as a Finn, which saved trouble with the Immigration people, who, because of the Revolution, were suspicious of all Russians and might have handed him over to the police.

This new character was a complete stranger and at the time I was under the impression that he was a friend of the big man. From subsequent experience of the type, I was able later to place him in his proper category. He was just a bum, one of the tribe of parasites who haunt ships and seamen when they are signing on or paying off. They usually have a couple of stolen paper discharges to bolster their claim to be fellow-seamen, firemen, or whatever. They seldom work, except to put in half a day occasionally as casual dock labourers and they will steal anything lying about a ship, providing it is portable, from razors, watches and money, to clothing which they can wear to make their exit from the dock estate.

The Russian opened a big bottle of beer and a flat half-bottle of whisky and offered me a choice while his companion filled an enamelled mug with beer and swallowed some of the whisky straight from the bottle. I smilingly declined the offer and though my shipmate was satisfied with my attitude, the other fellow was not.

'Ye'll no drink beer, laddie?' he asked, lurching towards my bunk and peering up at me.

'Whit's 'marrer wi 'oour beer? Wud ye sooner hae whusky?'

I tried to explain that I did not drink and that I did not like the smell of beer. Reaching up he thrust the cup against my lips which I kept tightly closed. His hand wavered and the cup was withdrawn then thrust back at my face, so that some of the contents splashed and ran down my cheeks. I received my baptism of beer right then and there and I did not care for the taste of it at all. Later I found it to be an acquired taste.

I saw anger mount in the man's eyes as he continued to press the cup against my closed lips, but by bending far back I avoided the thrust of his hand. The big Russian came to the rescue by declaring, 'All right, he don' want it, so leave the boy be. We have plenty for us together, ey?' The fat man listened to the voice of reason and the pair of them settled down side by side on the bench beside the table, to drink and talk and drink.

I listened to their conversation but it failed to interest me so undressing, I slid beneath the blankets and slept. I was awakened by a chorus of drunken song as new arrivals returned aboard in twos and threes and argued, drank from bottles and stumbled against the table, the seachests and each other. As the din died down I would close my eyes and be on the verge of unconsciousness when a fresh burst of quavering melody would roll round the lamp-lit fo'c'sle. Scottish songs vied with the folk music of Norway, Sweden, Finland, Denmark, Russia and Ireland. Several of the seamen were taking turns to play the new accordion and, drunk or not, they made a fair job of it.

They were nearly all drunk and glad to be in that state. One exception of course was the 'queerfeller' in the dark bottom bunk athwartships, Jesuschrist. Several of the young Scottish seamen had elected to remain at home for this last night of course. They would rejoin in the morning. Most of the seamen had gone ashore with the sole object of having a good time, like a hearty breakfast before a hanging, and intoxicating liquor was the mainstay of their entertainment.

Their lives were hard and dangerous, the rewards meagre and the living conditions not much improved in 150 years. Drunkenness was a very necessary part of their lives, easing and relaxing the tensions built up by hard, punishing work, risks taken, frustrated ambitions and the prolonged spells of abstinence from women.

Slowly the fo'c'sle settled down as the singing and argument grew less. One by one the men found their way into the bunks, or were picked off the deck and assisted into them by others. The accordion was returned to its case and the lamp wick lowered but from time to time I would be disturbed by some fellow-seaman threshing about and groaning and coughing in restless uneasy sleep, or by someone turning out to answer nature's call, which he would do in the scuppers outside my port and with a coughing spit over the side would cannon and bump his way inside again, to roll into his bunk with a creaking crash and sigh his way into blissful unconsciousness.

CHAPTER FIVE

A Tow Down the Clyde
to the Wind

This was the day! The day I had dreamed and schemed for, over so many years. Sailing Day. The 12th July, 1921. The Moment of Departure. The Voyage into the Future. The Gateway to Freedom! I had whispered these slogans so many times to myself that now they had overtaken me I didn't know what to do with them, or how they fitted my present circumstances. Still, I knew now that for the rest of my life I would stand on my own feet. Make my own decisions. Go where I wanted to go. Do what I wished to do. Be responsible for, *myself*! Or so I imagined.

When we all turned to at six o'clock I had the impression that the decks were full of men, like some paintings of deck scenes on old sailing men-of-war. Both the mates were out on deck and they were running their eyes over the newcomers while issuing instructions to the Bo'sun and the sailor who had been picked to act as bo'sun's mate. What had been said in the Consulate office about not carrying a bo'sun on this voyage, must have been over-ruled later, probably by a protest of the officers to the Master.

We were all split up into groups of twos and threes and sent about our work. I was struck by the way that some of the new men, when told by the Bo'sun to perform some particular job, would nod, perhaps give a slight hitch to their trousers or scratch a cheek or pass the back of their wrist across their nostrils and move away without a question or the least hesitation. These were the men who knew their business. Others, green hands, would stare blankly or question their neighbour, or turn and walk purposefully away in the wrong direction, to be recalled and redirected.

After a good breakfast we turned to again at various kinds of work. First, we singled up the mooring lines and wire springs. Owing to the great windage aloft of masts, yards, running and standing rigging, a sailing vessel is made fast to the quay by double the number of lines required to moor a steamship of similar tonnage. These now had to be reduced in number, so that when the time came to leave the wharf the ship would not be unduly delayed by having to let go and take in a profusion of mooring ropes and wires. The day was quite windless, however, so most of the lines were taken aboard. While we did this heavy work, some of the able seamen were bringing down to the pins on the mainrail, clewlines and buntlines which had been coiled down in the tops to save them from chafe or damage while the vessel was in port.

I was helping two other boys who were coiling the mooring ropes across the 'tweendeck beams. I was stationed under the fo'c'sle-head and was dragging heavy ropes towards me from the direction of the open main deck and passing the long lengths down the forehatch to the boys below. Other mooring ropes were coming off the steam-winch drum-ends above and straight down the hatch. The ship was fitted with four steam-winches, the power being supplied by a donkey boiler in the midship deck-house. This boiler was always shut down when the vessel put to sea and was not again used until the ship was on soundings near the land of her destination. While at sea the vessel was worked entirely by manpower, or as the seamen named it 'Armstrong's Patent'.

Another job I was put to was helping to get the old stockbroker's luggage aboard. This consisted of a couple of suitcases, a black wooden box and about 14 cases of whisky! As these cases reached the deck there were many ribald comments from the seamen, many of whom were suffering hangovers. However, all that they received in return were admonitions, 'Easy with that lot!' 'Don't drop them so hard!' 'Careful, careful!' This personal luggage was got aboard under strict security, watched by the Second Mate and the Steward, as though it contained gold bars being loaded into the Mint.

All hands went to dinner at noon. The ship was ready to leave port. It was a bright and sunny day with not a breath of wind to stir the folds of the large, clean, Norwegian ensign hanging limply at the high staff at the taffrail. This ensign staff was an enormous thing and was stepped in a swivelling socket bolted to the deck. It was a relic of *Lancing*'s days as a passenger liner on the North Atlantic–Mexico run when the flag would have to be visible above an awning. The seamen made jokes about it, saying that if a spanker or driver were set on it, the ship would become a five-masted barque.

The lack of wind caused some growling and speculation amongst the more experienced seamen as they consumed a satisfactory dinner of vegetable soup, corned meat and potatoes and fruit grut, in the fo'c'sle. They wondered how far the tug would tow us. Some said Pladda, others the north of Ireland. One or two said that we would anchor outside and wait for a wind, while another school of thought figured pessimistically that we would be 'beatin' an' driftin'' about the Firth of Clyde, 'haulin' them bloody great yards around like we wus in the Doldrums!'

While we were still at dinner a small tug arrived and made fast to our port side, abaft the mizzen rigging. The size of the tug proved conclusively to the holders of the Doldrum theory that we would not be towed very far. 'What did we tell yer! Now oo's right?'

The tug's name was *Queen*, she was a single-screw steamer, and, as events proved later, quite suitable for her present job. Her overall length was about 70 feet.

We were soon called out on deck and I saw a strange man wearing a soft hat and an overcoat, talking to the Chief Mate, Mr Larsen. They were standing beside the small inboard gangway ladder. I heard that he was the Scottish pilot. Meanwhile, our work consisted of moving fenders along the ship's side to better positions, under the instructions of whatever able seaman happened to be with us. The boys' work at this time seemed to be to follow the seamen around, helping them to the best of our ability in whatever work they were engaged on.

By this time my hands were sore and tender with the hard, unaccustomed work which I performed. Hauling on ropes which now felt prickly and hairy and which did not fit the small size of my hands, lifting and carrying cases of provisions which drove wood splinters into my fingers, emptying sacks of potatoes and coal and dragging sails about, which I could not lift because they were too heavy. All this had taken toll of the palms of my hands and fingers and I suffered every time I grasped anything firmly, even a mug of coffee. Shyly I mentioned this to my shipmates and they, without exception, advised me to resort to the use of personal urine! They said that this treatment would harden any pair of hands. They explained in some detail that navvies and firemen in steamers, resorted to this after a spell of unemployment had rendered their hands too soft for the shovel. Of course I refused to believe them, guessing that they were advocating a treatment which would make me look a damn fool. More leg-pulling, I thought. Blackbeard later advised me,

'Salt water, boy. That will give you a tough skin and in a couple of weeks your hands will be as hard as the rest of 'em!' He never used my other names. His mode of address to deck boys was the same as that of the mates, 'Boy!'

Now the Captain came out of the cabin with his son, Thorvald, the boy who was sailing with us, Mrs Pedersen and two other members of her family, who were, I think, daughters, for Mrs Pedersen called one of them 'Florence'. They were pretty girls dressed in white frocks with some kind of flowered-pattern trimmings and wore large floppy wide-brimmed hats. With the Captain they all walked towards the high bulwarks beyond which lay the tug. Mrs Pedersen was the last to leave the ship and, while her husband was chatting to the Master of the *Queen*, she was fussing over her son, giving him last minute instructions regarding wet socks, changing his underwear, his dirty knees, his boots and telling him to be sure to go to bed at nine o'clock! I could not actually hear what was said to him but *I knew*! She probably warned him to keep away from the sailors in the fo'c'sle too, and I viewed this performance with the contempt which I thought it deserved.

Secretly, I felt mighty relieved that my mother had not appeared to demonstrate her affection for me and wave me good-bye. Of course *he* was only a kid of 14 wearing short pants and, of all things to put to sea with, his school cap! He even wore the thing during the voyage. While his mother fussed over him and gave him a last desperate hug and kiss, as mothers usually do at parting, he seemed quite unconcerned

and did not appear to me to be ashamed of it all, as I would
have been.

The dog had joined in the farewells too and was jumping
around with wagging tail, licking hands, and barking with
lowered head and upthrust snout at the two seamen, who were
standing by to lower the small gangway back aboard the tug.
They were not used to dogs and were not at all sure that it
would not take a lump out of them. Or so they said later.

The *Queen*, with her load of passengers cluttering up her
bridgedeck, cast off. Our shore gangway was hoisted aboard,
the Pilot, Captain and Second Mate with some of the hands
appeared on the poop as the rest of us moved forward under
the fo'c'sle-head. The tug had slid ahead and her stern was
under our clipper bow so we payed out the tow-rope through
the starboard towing hawse-pipe and, on a shout from the deck
of the tug, made it fast on the ship's bitts. (The ship was fitted
with double hawse-pipes cast as a single unit, and not hawse-
holes as in other sailing ships.)

Leaving the Carpenter and a seaman to slack the tow-rope
when required, we made our way up to the fo'c'sle-head where
the old Mate was supervising the taking in of the last rope holding the bow to the Kilmarnock No. 1 berth of the Eglington
Dock.

Very slowly the gap of water between the ship and the quay
widened and the coal dust and the broken bits of dunnage wood
floating on the surface spun and twisted in the faint sucking
currents. I was told to stand on the t'gallant rail and to steer
a fender between the ship's side and the knuckle of the pier if
they came too close. I was warned not to lose the fender, but
nothing was said about falling over the side and losing my life.

Standing there, lanyard in hand, I watched the shoreline slip
slowly away as we passed the cranes, the railway engines and
trucks, a coaster discharging cement and the background of the
squat buildings ashore. One or two people gave us a wave of
the hand in farewell but I was too lofty and important to reply.
I thought that was kid's stuff, like the traditional wavings to
the passengers of a passing train. I was yet to learn and
appreciate a friendly gesture from a stranger. These people
probably knew what we were in for 'across the Western Ocean'.
I didn't!

The ship slowly passed between the pier-heads, keeping closer to Lighthouse Pier than to the breakwater until, nearing a red buoy, the tug altered course to the southward, and we all got the benefit of a wave of sulphurous smoke and fumes from her funnel. A small island that lay to starboard gradually swung around until it was astern and I was informed by another of the deck boys that it was Horse Isle. He did not know why. However, a seaman told me, 'That was once the lair of the Greenock Pirates who used to raid Ardrossan in thick fog and carry off the women and young girls, an' any other loot they could lay their hands on, like money an' scrap iron and 'orses!'

My ears stretched and I liked my lips, this was an explanation after my own heart and I believed him until someone laughed and I saw other grins. Then I was worried, and not for the first time. When would I learn truth from falsehood, know when I was being kidded? How long would it be before I had a proper understanding of men's minds? In short, how long was it going to take me to grow up?

The ship was towed slowly south, down the Firth of Clyde, heading towards Ailsa Craig with the low-lying coast of Ayrshire to port and the green hills of the Island of Arran to starboard. The afternoon wore on while we sweated at a variety of jobs and the weather remained calm and clear as the big ship moved through the glassy waters of the Firth. The smoke from the tug ahead rose straight up in a grey-black plume from her funnel then curved gently and gracefully east.

A whistle shrilled three quick blasts. The Chief Mate was descending the poop ladder preceded by the Second Mate who was calling on all hands to man the braces and swing the yards around. Since I did not understand the language I had to listen for the translation always given to us by some of the other seamen in English, until we had a grasp of most of the usual Norwegian phrases shouted at us. We were about to make sail. Now I would see what a ship under sail looked like, from her decks!

When the yards had been braced for a westerly wind on the starboard beam we were ordered aloft to the topsail yards. The Chief Mate sent the ordinary seamen and boys nearest to him up the fore and mainmasts while the Second Mate chased me up the mizzen with another boy. I think he was aware that I knew what to do when I was up there but an able seaman followed us and laid out on the yard too.

We cast the gaskets off the lower topsail as quickly as we could and let them hang there. We would make them up later in coils as we descended from the upper yards. The seaman stayed to let go the bunt gasket while we cast off the gaskets of the upper topsail then climbed to the t'gallant yards. As we progressed upwards to the royal yard, the deck below us resounded to the hauling cries of the seamen as they sheeted home the sails we had loosed. The whole rigging quivered and shook as the halliards brought the upper topsail, upper t'gallant and royal yards to the limit of their hoist. I was not yet to see what a sailing ship looked like from her decks!

I was on the weather, or starboard, side of the lower topsail yard and engaged in making up gaskets when I heard whistles sounding from the region of our decks and which appeared to be answered by the steam whistle of the tug ahead which now sheered to starboard, still towing. A faint wind had been blowing but, because of the movement of the ship, it went unnoticed by me.

The tug slowed down and the tow-rope sagged through the water in a graceful rippling curve. I think that the skipper of the tug was under the impression that *Lancing* would also slow down, but even with this light wind in her sails she kept on going. She did not act like the kind of vessels that he was used to. The tow-rope skipped along the surface, decreasing its curve and becoming a straight line between the bows of the full-rigged ship and the funnel casing of the tug which was now nearly abeam and steering the same course. Then the tow-rope lifted clear of the sea and spun and shivered along its length as the strain rapidly increased, throwing glistening showers of shed-water in circular halos, wide in the sunlight.

The tug heeled over to port, listing rapidly until water gushed on to her deck as her small scuppers and wash-ports were engulfed while she still had way through the sea. I heard screams and cries as I watched fascinated, and loud shouts of men from our decks. There came the sound of a dull thump and a clang of metal aboard the *Queen* and the tow-rope leaped away from her and swam rapidly back alongside us and disappeared from my view. The small tug swung back upright then rolled from side to side repeatedly while water gushed from her scuppers and wash-ports. She was safe now but it had nearly been a tragedy!

The *Queen* appeared to be drawn over about 20° within two or three seconds. As I watched, none of the small mass of people clustered about the funnel moved as she went over. They just hung on and remained still. If she had capsized they would all have gone with her. I suppose that the mate of the tug or the leading hand, who is usually stationed aft for just such an emergency, picked up a hammer and knocked out the well-greased pin, tripping the hook.

A loud hail from the deck caused me to look downwards and the seaman aloft with me called out that I was to get off the yard and into the rigging as the men below were manning the weather mizzen braces. He joined me at the mast as the mournful hauling cries of the seamen at the starboard mizzen braces commenced and the big yards began to move as a Mate slacked away the three lee braces on the opposite side of the ship.

'Get down on deck, son, afore yer knocked down!' The seaman's advice was sound and I stepped quickly along a sheer ratline until I reached the royal backstay, down which I slid rapidly. As I reached the rail a deep sighing and rustling enveloped me which suddenly changed into a cracking thunder of sails pointing into the wind with the harsh banging and ringing of chain sheets followed by the swift, creaking hush as the sounds ceased and all the sails on the mizzen curved flatly against the mast, all aback in the soft breeze. The ship slowed then stopped.

Pelle called to me from the vicinity of the jigger fife-rail on the poop so I joined him and helped to coil down, clear for running, the mizzen t'gallant and royal braces. This was a job which I was to perform times without number on all the braces in the ship. Each part of the manilla coil had to overlap slightly the previous coil so that a lapped effect was produced which prevented the brace kinking or fouling as the line uncoiled rapidly when slacked off. The finished coil was elliptical in shape and had rather a fancy and neat appearance as it lay on the deck, or the hatches or, during bad weather, on the tops of deck-houses or across lifeboat covers.

While engaged in this occupation the tug came alongside and the pilot boarded her, taking with him last-minute letters (some doubtless unstamped) and I have often thought since that the ships' pilots of the world must spend a pound or two each year paying postage on the correspondence of complete strangers, usually boys and apprentices, and trying sometimes to get rid of foreign coins.

The tug had squeezed herself into the wide gap on the ship's side, formed when the mizzen yards were laid aback. The mizzen yard-arm was nearly touching that of the main on the port side while the cro'jack yard-arm was poking at the mizzen on the starboard side. (The cro'jack, or cross jack, was the lowest square sail on the jigger mast.) I was too busy to notice much of what went on but there were loud voices and shrill voices calling back and forth and hands waving, laughter and smiles brought to a crescendo by the whirring jangle of a steamer's telegraph bell, shouts of, 'Let go!' and 'All gone, sir!' followed by the strangled, watery hooting of the tug's whistle, a dog barking in excitement and the sudden boil of white, frothing water under the broad counter of the small *Queen* as she cleared our side and moved away, to come to a stop about half a cable's length off the beam.

I stayed where I was and helped to haul on the mizzen upper braces as the yards were again brought round, the sails filled with wind and the ship gathered way once more. When next I saw the *Queen* she was steaming parallel with us and I saw a man in a grey suit pointing a camera in our direction.

The foresail came down from the fore yard with a rush and a whirring of patent block sheaves and the sheet and tack brought home. The heavy storm canvas was wrinkled like a piece of tripe after its period of security in tight gaskets on the yard. We set the jigger topmast staysail and moved to the rail to look at the tug but she was falling behind now as our speed increased. The last I saw of her she was casting towards our counter and, with a series of weak blasts from her steam whistle, made a wide sweep and turned for home. Our ensign was dipped in reply while the Captain, his young son and Mr Martin, the other passenger, waved hands in a final farewell, but by this time I was busy again on the main yard.

CHAPTER SIX

Learning the Ropes

The tug had left us off Corsewall Point at the entrance to Loch Ryan and shortly after we manned the braces again and, starting with the fore yards, hauled away until the yards were nearly touching the lee shrouds and backstays as the course of the ship was altered, and as the orders came, 'Belay that'. Then, 'Coil down the running gear'. The bowsprit was pointing south. I knew then that the preliminaries were over. The ship was at sea.

While we boys were coiling down the lines clear for running the seamen were 'fishing' the two bower anchors. By means of the crane mounted on the fore part of the fo'c'sle-head they were bringing the heavy anchors inboard and lowering them into position on the deck where they would remain, resting on removable wood blocks shaped to the flukes and lashed down with chains, until the ship picked up the coast of North America.

It was early yet, I gathered, to secure the anchors on the deck, for this operation is usually performed when the ship is clear of the land and judged to be free of any emergencies which might entail anchoring. I think that Captain Pedersen felt that the job were better done now, while we were still within sheltered waters. To get the anchors aboard later, while the vessel was rolling and plunging in the swell of the North Atlantic, would entail considerable effort, skill and risk to life and limb because the weight of each anchor was in the neighbourhood of three and a half tons. To have that ponderous menace suspended over a heaving deck and at the same time control it would cause a tremendous amount of hard, dangerous work. I had an opportunity later to inspect the anchor crane at close quarters when I assisted one of the seamen to grease the bushes of the block sheaves after the crane was dismantled and the fish-tackle was unrove. The brass sheaves were the largest in the ship, fully 14 or 15 inches in diameter, larger than that in the topsail halliard blocks. I think too, that stowing the anchors was brought forward because steam was still available to the winch on the fo'c'sle-head.

The ship was sailing close-hauled towards the Irish Sea and I and three other deck-boys were beckoned to the side of the Second Mate who produced from the pockets of his khaki uniform, several small bundles of sail twine. Opened out and separated they were revealed as bunches of short lengths of string about 50 to a bundle, six inches long, secured loosely in the middle. We were told that these were buntline stops and were instructed in the manner of their use and misuse. Then the four of us were ordered aloft, one to each mast, to put the brief lesson into practice.

Tying my little sail twine bundle to my belt (I later preferred to secure them to the top buttonhole of my shirt), I started up the lower rigging of the foremast. Reaching the fore yard I moved out on the lee side and commenced by trying to overhaul the nearest buntline.

Buntlines are manila ropes which lead from the sail to the deck where they are made fast. Their purpose is to gather the sail up to the yard when the sheets are let go and so control it while it is being furled, or taken in. An ordinary Venetian blind is equipped with similar lines or cords, which perform the same function by gathering the louvres upwards to the top of a window. When a sail is properly set, the buntlines lie slackly down the front of the sail with a small bight or loop of line swinging free below the foot. If the buntlines were not slack they would soon cause a bad chafe on the canvas and ultimately weaken the fabric until a hole or split appeared. Reinforcing cloths are sewn to the sail where the buntline will touch it.

However, *Lancing*'s buntlines were wire ropes, shackled to a manila whip at the mast. Sometimes we would put the stops on this whip but usually we stopped the wire itself to the yard jackstay.

Up on the fore yard I struggled with the wire buntline but could not get any slack until it dawned on me that I had omitted to let it go on deck before I climbed aloft. I had thought that someone else would do it. Perhaps the Second Mate? Descending to the deck I found that everyone was too busy working to give heed to my questions or point out to me the lines which should be cast off the belaying pins. Aside from the braces, halliards and topsail sheets, I did not know one line from another or where in the ship they were made fast.

I moved about from fife-rail to rigging, pulling and tugging on random ropes and following each aloft with my eyes in order to discern which one moved. This was not successful as the movement of the sails and pressure of wind, stronger now, caused all the slack ropes to move.

Engaged in this useless pursuit, I was interrupted by the Cook who must have been watching me. He showed me the right lines, where they were belayed and helped me to throw the coils down on the deck and cast the lines off the pins. 'You make them up again, when you come down. Don' forget!' He smacked the palms of his big hands loudly together. 'Or Mister Larsen he will be ver' angry. You will get no watch below for one week!' As I stepped from the fo'c'sle-head into the lee rigging and started aloft again he called out some urgent advice about learning the ropes *fast*!

When deck boys and ordinary seamen are carried in a sailing ship, it is their job to 'stop the buntlines' and I found that there is no better way of learning the run of the gear than by doing this job and taking an interest in it. Back on the fore yards I successfully stopped each buntline and the royal leechlines, 25 lines in all.

As the early stages of the voyage progressed, we boys were shown by the seamen the run of the gear and we learned the various positions in the ship where the lines were brought down and belayed, but it took us much longer to learn the Norwegian names for the sails and gear simply because the seamen knew the English names and explained in both languages. They had all sailed in British and American ships.

Braces, sheets and halliards were easily identified because they were comparatively few in number and recognized by their size and prominent positions and could be traced aloft by eye. They were always named in commands: 'Main upper t'gallant halliards' or 'Lee fore brace', when checking the yards in as the wind drew ahead, and 'Weather cro'jack brace' as the wind came astern and the yards had to be squared in order to take full advantage of it.

The sheets and tacks of the big courses and that of the lower topsails were also easily recognized so that when the order came, 'Lee foresheet', or 'Weather tack down', we knew instantly what was wanted. One very soon got to know the tacks of the square sails because *Lancing* was not equipped with main deck capstans, with which to wind in the sheets and tacks, other than the big capstan on the fo'c'sle-head. All the sheets and tacks of the main and mizzen courses had to be hove down by means of a tack-tackle which was made up of two two-fold blocks and manilla rope. This tackle was usually kept in the bo'sun's locker and had to be brought on deck when it was required.

This tackle was the deck boy's curse. When the tack had been hove down by the combined efforts of all the watch, the tackle was hooked into the clew-spectacle and the lower block to a ringbolt or a bulwark stanchion. It was usually my job to shin up the tack and guide the heavy hook into the clew-iron while three panting seamen held the block up towards me. Frequently I had my fingers jammed as the ship took a roll and the seamen swayed away from me in the dark of night or when a boarding sea hit them.

We boys found that the maze of lines, blocks and wires were based on a definite plan or system which had evolved as the sailing vessel had increased in size over the centuries. It was all based on sound common sense and a determined conservative policy not to change the name of anything, so as to avoid confusion. So far as I know, it is an international system outside of all politics and has never been agreed to or even discussed by any national group. Any skilled seaman of any nation can board any sailing ship of any nationality and in pitch darkness put his hand on and name any rope, line, block, brace or halliard in that ship. There are small variations of course, especially in schooners, but in all essential details the system is standard.

The sun was low when I came down from aloft and we had a hurried late meal before mustering aft on the starboard side of the deck, under the boat skids. We were all assembled in a large crescent-shaped group and the two Mates proceeded to pick the watches.

66

The Chief Mate pointed to one man and the seaman stepped away and stood near the jigger hatch. Then the Second Mate did likewise and his man left the group and moved further away, to stand against the main rail. So it proceeded, a finger pointed and men moved away to port and starboard.

I had heard and read of this selection business and I knew that the mates always tried to get the best seamen into their own watches, so the best men went first. As the weeding out went on I began to worry and edged myself nearer the front as I wanted to go in the starboard watch. The Second Mate I knew, but I was not too sure about the Chief Mate. He seemed to keep all boys on the move and performing dirty jobs.

The able seamen and one ordinary seaman had been picked and a couple of the bigger deck boys had moved away so I was really anxious. The Second Mate, bless his penetrating insight and his knowledge of a good man, pointed at me and with an overwhelming feeling of relief and gladness I stepped smartly away and joined my watchmates of the starboard watch. I was quick to count the numbers left behind me. There were four! For that I was very thankful. Out of the 19 men and boys, the Mate got the odd one and nobody begrudged him his advantage. It just happened to be Jesuschrist.

Pelle, Larvik, Stavanger, Blackbeard, the Farmer, the Schoolmaster, the big Russian and some others whose names or nicknames I have forgotten were all in my watch, together with a negro, black as the inside of a seaboot. Born of West Indian parents in, I think, Greenock, he was of average height, slim and about 25 years of age. A good seaman with a happy and willing disposition, he would go out of his way to perform a kindly action for any one of us. A good shipmate. Even when tempers flared there was no sign of any colour discrimination. We were all one, thrown together by chance or individual choice and all mucked in together. The black Scotsman was nicknamed 'Whitey' and sometimes 'Snowy'.

When the watches had been picked, the Chief Mate ordered his watch to go below, while the Second Mate instructed us to keep handy. We returned to the fo'c'sle which had seen little of us during the day. As the men of the port watch prepared to turn in the Farmer made a suggestion. It was that we should keep the same bunks we now occupied, since, '. . . it will be a short voyage anyhow!' This was agreed to, and the business of changing over to another bunk and moving seachests around, was no longer necessary. It is the custom in a sailing ship for the port watch to use the port side of the fo'c'sle while the starboard watch occupied the other side when the fo'c'sle is one single space and not two separate areas. The advantage of this is in the early days of a voyage when a crew is brought aboard within an hour of sailing and all are strangers to each other and remain so for a number of watches, at the change of watches it is then safe to call all the men on one side of the fo'c'sle.

The entrance of the Bo'sun and his mate put the final seal on the day's labours. They had come to allocate the 'wheels' and 'look-outs' in consultation with the able seamen. It was all over in five minutes. I found that I would be on lookout on the fo'c'sle-head from ten o'clock to midnight.

In *Lancing*, all look-outs were shared by able seamen, ordinary seamen and deck boys, for this was a short-handed ship. I still think that to put a boy in such a responsible position as part-guardian of the safety of a ship, is a short-sighted policy. It was now about nine o'clock and I was exhausted with the heavy work of sailing day. The Bo'sun's Mate spoke, 'All right, watch on deck—out on deck!' I looked longingly and lovingly at my bunk as the lamp wick was lowered and we moved out to the dark shelter of the bo'sun's locker.

A shore light was flashing far out on the port beam. One of the seamen said that it was the Calf of Man. The Donkeyman was in our watch and he became the 'policeman'. He was the man who patrolled the decks at night and answered the summons of the Mate's whistles; he was, in fact, the stand-by man. The remainder of the watch on deck curled up in odd corners and yarned, dozed or slept until called by the police-man for a wheel, a look-out or for some particular task, or general sail handling ordered by the officer on watch. I was sur-prised that an experienced seaman should volunteer for such a job while his shipmates slept. Doubtless there were compensations.

About five of us, including the Bo'sun's Mate, chose the locker as the most comfortable place to rest while we were on deck. This was a fairly large store-room under the fo'c'sle-head on the starboard side with its doorway facing the forehatch.

The contents consisted of coils of manila' and wire ropes, steel and wood blocks, the portable fog-horn and all the spare rigging gear such as shackles, hardwood and steel sheaves, chain ties, mast-head gantlines and masses of galvanized iron thimbles, rigging screws and other things, a great amount of which were hanging from horizontal rods fixed to the ship's side and the bulkheads. Many ropes and wires were coiled on the wood gratings which covered the iron deck. This locker was flanked, on the afterpart, by a lamp-locker and on the forepart by a lavatory, both of whose iron doors opened outwards under the fo'c'sle-head.

The locker smelled of Stockholm tar, rope preservative oils and wet wood and, as I found out later, it was a comfortable place in which to shelter from the wind, the driving rain or spray and the seas which sometimes swept the whole main deck. There was no form of artificial lighting in any of these spaces, with the exception of the small kerosene lamp in the fo'c'sle, and during the hours of darkness lavatories and lockers were as black as pitch, unless the moon or stars exerted their influence on the glassed ports.

We stumbled inside, felt our way around and sank down wearily into coils of soft rope. The iron door was left open for ventilation. Over-tired bodies relaxed painfully, some slept and snored while others talked in low tones with long pauses between question and answer.

'What wus yer lass ship, Bose?' Silence. Then the throat of the Bo'sun's Mate began to clear itself. A match flared in cupped hands for a brief instant as a cigarette drew down the flame. Another voice, 'Mind 'at bloody light will yer!' Came the reply to the question. '*Metagama*—"the blood-boat" of the Western Ocean,' a long sigh. Silence. The questioner observed, 'Huh, passenger ship, get yer watch-below in them ships all right.' Another long pause, then the reply cut through the darkness. 'She wus full o' razor-slashers. They called 'emselves Redskins. Gutter 'ooligans!' This was in reference to a notorious gang of Glasgow hooligans. They and other gangs tried to bring a reign of terror to the city, their victims shop-keepers and other innocents. When police pressure became too severe for them they would ship out as firemen in the liners or skip to Northern Ireland.

A darker shadow appeared at the pale rectangle of the doorway and a whiff of strong tobacco smoke entered as a hoarse voice spoke. 'Yack, you dare? Your look-out!' I rose stiffly, aching with tiredness, groped and stumbled to the doorway. I was never to hear of the stirring slaughters in 'the blood boat', for when questioned later, the Bo'sun's Mate avoided all direct answers, usually by giving me some dirty job to perform. I took the hint. I think he was rather ashamed to admit that he had shipped in a passenger liner. In those days, seamen referred to their crews as, 'ex-navymen and bums'. A seaman was reckoned to be pretty hard-up to ship in one of them.

Moving out on deck I felt that the wind was gaining in strength and climbing the ladder to the fo'c'sle-head I was unprepared for the force of wind spilling down from the foot of the foresail; it caught me and made me stagger. Looking forward I saw two dark figures outlined against the lighter sky. They were standing near the knight-heads, talking.

As I approached them the thin sound of four bells striking was borne to us from aft. One of the look-outs broke away and passed me on his way to answer the notes of the bell but as he reached the upturned longboat on top of the forward house, the big bell nearby was lightly struck by the hand of the policeman while the other look-out man roared out, 'All-l-l-s Well-l-l!' The first man returned, peered closely into my face, muttered, 'Yack', and descended the ladder to the main deck on his way to report my name to the officer on watch for inclusion in the log-book. Another shadowy figure mounted to the deck and relieved the other look-out man. Double look-outs were being maintained while the ship was passing down the Irish Sea. The newcomer who joined me was revealed as Blackbeard.

While the two of us were straining our eyes into the darkness ahead and abeam we were joined by the Second Mate who told us, in English, that we must watch for fishing vessels, such as drifters, which might have their nets out poaching without lights. He also warned us to watch the waters nearer the ship for dark floating objects which looked like rocks and could sometimes be seen when a wave crest broke over them or a sea-bird flew off them. These would probably be drifting mines and we were to yell our heads off and strike the bell furiously if we saw one!

I hoped that I would see and report a mine. Perhaps we would even be sunk by one! On the homeward run of course, I did not know then the power of a mine, so the thought thrilled me. I visualized the headlines: 'SURVIVORS OF THE NORWEGIAN SAILING SHIP *Lancing* LAND AT GLASGOW'.

The Second Mate inspected the fore-tack and the jib and staysail sheets, looked over each bow at the anchor cables still in place and, after a long gaze aloft at the silent sails on the foremast, left us to look for lights and dark shapes while he rejoined the Captain on the poop.

*　　　*　　　*

Owing to my age, the War had passed me by and I was sad at the thought that now I was starting my life in earnest I would never have the opportunity to be an officer of a famous regiment, such as the Camerons or the Black Watch, and fight with others in the 51st Division, leading a charge across the machine-gun-swept waste of no-man's-land, or piloting a fighter aircraft of the Royal Flying Corps, equipped with twin-Vickers, firing through the propeller and watching my enemy plunge flaming to earth far below, before turning my attention to another six aircraft.

These were a scant couple of my boyhood dreams and now that I had become a man and was doing a man's job, or so I thought, I would perforce have to abandon, since the Great War was over. My pre-military training had been brief and enjoyable as a cadet in the School Corps. In winter we had drilled in the hall of the 5th Scottish Rifles and in summer spent two weeks training in a military camp at Gales, close to Troon, in Ayrshire. This camp was really a large military training area whose terrain was modelled on important enemy targets chosen for future attacks. But when we reached it the victories had been won.

We exercised in the trenches, strong-points and the sandbag replica of the Hindenburg Redoubt fortress and returned each night with our loot of cartridge cases and unarmed Mills grenades. We, and a strong platoon of the W.A.A.C., were billeted in huts but the Canadian and Australian troops were under canvas nearby, and a wild lot they all were. Especially the women's corps. The Aussies fought the Canucks when opportunity offered and love and war being such close companions, coupled with the presence of the women freedom-fighters, the enemy strong-points and dugouts were littered with the debris of love. Gales and Troon golfcourse were sights I shall long remember.

Each day we were marched to the nearby beach for swimming exercise where there was a wooden, grey-painted barque driven ashore, bows on. There looked to be nothing the matter with her as she stood upright in the shallows about 300 feet from the dry sand. One of our officers said that the artillery were going to use her for target practice. It seemed a terrible waste. And what about all the sharp wood splinters which would litter our beach? We returned home before destruction commenced, but I would have liked to have spent my holidays aboard her.

*   *   *

Some of the watch on deck were restless, probably at the thoughts of drifting mines, because there were still a few about even in 1921. So two of the men had joined us, lending two more pairs of eyes to the search of the dark waters.

My eyes were untrained to pick out faint lights at far distances and with continual straining into darkness I began to see pinpoints of light wherever I looked. Blackbeard, crouching low on the deck beside me, so as to see under the bowsprit and the headgear, said, 'Well, it *might* be a light, because your eyes are younger than mine, but I think we will wait until we all see it!' We saw nothing except what had already been reported, three distant steamers and two sailing vessels and the flashing loom of a light on low cloud far away off the weather bow, which they said was the Skerries, or maybe it was Howth, on the coast of Ireland; they were not sure which.

My two hours' look-out passed quickly for I was mentally refreshed by our instructions, with the interest aroused by thoughts of illegal fishing and the menace of drifting mines, to say nothing of the interesting snippets of conversation going on around me, some of which I understood when voiced in English. My shipmates spoke of the heavy weather they had encountered in other ships when making a passage down this same Irish Sea.

Blackbeard gave me a piece of sound advice on the observation of lights and objects at far distances. 'If you think you see something, take a bearing on it by the cloud-shape, the stars or the sun, then do not look directly at it. Look above and below and to either side, for you will probably see it plainer then and be able to identify it.'

One bell was struck by the policeman in answer to the after bell and instantly pandemonium broke loose in the fo'c'sle deck-house. Full-throated shouts, yells and the banging of tin plates on the table and bunkboards was the normal method of calling the watch in this full-rigged ship. In all other vessels I served in later, both British and Colonial, calling the watch was a gentlemanly business. Not so in *Lancing*! However, it had the desired effect. Everyone awoke and were on their feet in various stages of fury, shock and rank bad temper, instantly prepared for work, murder or *felo de se*; eventually one became used to it.

On the first double stroke of eight bells the watch below tumbled out of the fo'c'sle and together with the watch on deck hurried aft to be counted and accounted for. Normally in sailing vessels, the port watch would assemble in a group on the port side of the main deck at the break of the poop while the starboard watch would do the same on the opposite side. In this ship, however, we did not follow the pattern.

Both watches gathered on the weather side near the double poop ladders while the Bo'sun peered and counted and the Bo'sun's Mate ran his eyes over his chickens, tender and tough. Then satisfied, the Bo'sun's Mate called to the Bo'sun, 'All 'ere, two on look-out, one to the wheel!' Then the Bo'sun cried in a clear strong voice to the two figures of the Mates, silhouetted above on the poop, 'Watches aft, sir!' Back down came the Norwegian equivalent for 'All right. Relieve the wheel and look-outs!' And maybe with some instruction or order added: 'Keep handy the watch', or 'Clew the mainsail up!'

In bad weather we would assemble in the lee alleyway of the poop deckhouse instead of on the open and exposed main deck. This assembly business was common to all sailing ships but was never a routine in steamers. The purpose of it was twofold. First, to make sure that the watch were really out on deck and ready when required. Secondly, to reassure the officer that we were, one and all, still aboard the ship and had not fallen over the side unnoticed, or had been murdered and dumped over, had deserted, or were in concealment down in the hold, such as a man deciding to savour the bliss of an unbroken night's sleep, trusting that he would not be missed at the change of watches in a blacked-out ship.

Blackbeard and I were duly relieved on the look-out. It was now our turn to go below and relaxed and thankful we entered the warm fo'c'sle. Divesting myself of my shoes, which I dropped into the wedge-shaped space between two seachests, I hung my trousers on a nail driven into the bunk stanchion and rolled wearily in. The fact that my trousers were off at last gave me a complete sense of comfort and ease. Pulling the two blankets over my chest I lay back luxuriously on my straw bed and stared up at the white painted planks of the deck-head, about 30 inches above my face.

As I watched nothing and cared nothing the only remaining active part of me seemed to be my ears. The aches and pains of the day clamoured for recognition and found none, for I was far too exhausted. The brief conversations around me died away as the lowering lamp wick brought the shadows rushing upwards and inwards while the sounds of the wind in the rigging, the slap of small seas on the iron hull and the faint creaking of woodwork lulled the lead-heavy lids over my dulled eyes.

CHAPTER SEVEN

Work Aloft and Alow

At four o'clock in the morning I was dragged roughly from the depths of slumber in my warm, comfortable bunk and thrown to the deck only half-conscious. As the big bell commenced striking its eight double notes a hard hand slapped me across the face as I scrambled upright, then my trousers hit me on the chest and dropped to my feet. As I attempted to scramble into my pants I looked at the man who had hit me. It was the young Finnish able seaman. His blue eyes were blazing with temper while a stream of broken English abuse poured towards me from his twisted mouth. Half-way into my trousers I was caught in the torrent of men hurrying out to the deck, on their way to muster aft. Hopping and skipping I finally got into my pants as we passed the galley.

When we had all returned to the fo'c'sle I asked the Finn why he had hit me. In reply I received two or three more open-handed blows, one of which cut the inside of my mouth and I dribbled blood. Finally, he informed me that my crime consisted of remaining asleep in my bunk when called and not turning out at eight bells!

I trembled with hot fury and itched to punch the pale, lumpy face or hit him with something heavy that would really damage. Later, I even considered using my sheath knife on him, but he was broad and muscular and a grown man, while I was only a small boy and I sensed that if I did tear into him, he would not be able to control himself and would batter me unconscious, at the least!

I had known boys at school who went berserk. Them I could handle but this was a different proposition. This was an 11-stone man who, I could see, was dangerous to others. I resolved to watch my step with him because hate of me shone in his eyes and was reflected in his voice and manner. I was at a loss to understand why. True, I had slept in but this was not sufficient to arouse hatred. His attitude puzzled me and I did my best to avoid him. None of the other seamen in the fo'c'sle interfered with my punishment, so I assumed that I had sinned against the code and deserved a hiding.

Some of the other deck boys brought their sympathy to me later and we reached the obvious conclusion that the young Finn was a real mean character, probably a bit mental, and would have to be avoided if possible. He was, of course, a bully, since one hard slap or a kick on the bottom would have served the purpose.

Conquering the desire for sleep was to be my greatest trouble during my early days at sea. Before the voyage ended I was able to resist closing my eyes when they should be open, but it was a hard struggle. Coming from a home where there was every comfort and not a few luxuries, I had had a room of my own, three servants were employed and a children's nurse, any of whom would awaken me in the mornings, two or three times! I had been spoiled and I was now discovering this fact of life. Of course, at home I had imagined that the odds were all against me, against a life of adventure. There I had been surrounded by comfort, good food and plenty of it, gas fires and security, and I wanted none of them. Here I was, with wind, wetness and brutality! I brooded.

The night was dark and moonless. Three blasts of the whistle brought us on deck and for an hour we sweated up the gear, hauling on braces, halliards and sheets. This was when the presence of a dog aboard was first felt. During the night it had discharged various cargoes on to the braces which were coiled down on the deck. It had also been sick on them. Lurid curses rent the air in several languages and the Second Mate ordered out hurricane lamps, brooms and buckets and the draw-bucket, then fully equipped we swept and scrubbed the various sticky deposits into the scuppers. *That bloody thing* was the subject of all conversations for the remaining two hours.

When daylight had whitened the grey sails we had looked for land but, aside from a dark smudge over the starboard quarter which might have been cloud or the Saltee Islands off the coast of Wexford, nothing was to be seen. The ship was pitching into a head sea and to reduce her speed slightly, for there was a job of work to be performed by the watch which would entail a man going over the bows; it had been decided to clew up the royals.

Pelle took me with him and when the sail had been brought to the yard we climbed aloft on the mainmast rigging. He was my instructor. He showed me how to furl a sail as he first made fast the bunt-gasket, then I was sent out on the lee side of the yard to put the lesson into practice while Pelle smothered and made fast the weather side of the sail which was ballooning and thrashing itself with sounds like whips against the yard, and him. It was doing the same on my side but not so violently. He completed his side and crossed over to help me pass and tighten the gaskets then we gathered at the mast to talk and look around. The royal yards were constructed of solid wood, unlike the iron and steel yards below us, and they were very old. I noticed gaps of up to nine inches in length where portions of the wooden jackstays, to which the head of the sail is bent, or made fast, were missing and had not been repaired, even temporarily.

After the morning wash down of the decks we started the job of unshackling the anchor cables and lowering them into the chain lockers. Every time the ship's bows went down a flood poured into the space under the fo'c'sle-head and with a deeper pitch huge squirts would hit the beams over the windlass and dollop down on top of us. Our seaboots were filled with cold, salt water and chilled feet. We managed to stow away one cable before we were relieved by the port watch, who observing our condition, had donned oilskins.

Next day, during the long afternoon watch on deck, I discovered a sure cure for seasickness. Near the fore rigging there was an inclined wooden garbage chute used for dumping rubbish and slops into the sea. It was portable and we changed it from one side to the other, depending on which was the lee side. This chute was thrust through the nearest wash-port in the bulwarks.

I had been told to take the empty dinner kits back to the galley, so nesting them in my arms, I staggered out on to the main deck. The decks were heaving and shuddering with the motion of the ship through the seas. Pausing at the chute I

77

emptied the left-overs which had been dumped into a single kit. The sloppy mess squelched down and bits of fat, potatoes, coffee grains, pea soup and gravy dripped and spread slowly like some greenish-yellow silent glacier. I was fascinated by the horror of it!

Suddenly I became conscious of the movement of the ship, something that I had taken for granted until this moment. I experienced a queasy fluttering as my stomach commenced to strain against its moorings. But the sudden blasts of the Second Mate's whistle brought me to my senses. I ran to the galley, thrust the kits inside the door coaming, leaving them on the deck then hastened to join my shipmates at the jigger royal buntlines.

'Haul away there!' cried the Bo'sun's Mate as he slacked away the royal halliards while three of us manned the clewlines, buntlines and leechlines on both sides of the ship and pulled and yelled with our treble voices. The Second Mate with others of the watch were clewing up the fore royal at the same time.

'Belay that—belay all!' shouted the Bo'sun's Mate and we quickly took a turn and hitched the lines to the pins. On his way to the mizzen fife-rail to assist the able seamen align the yard with the royal braces which had been tended as the yard came down the mast, he looked at me and with upraised forearm pointing a thick finger at the sky, growled,

'Aloft an' furl. See what kind of a mess *you* make of it!'

I reached the royal yard and as I battled alone with the billowing, thrashing canvas my incipient seasickness was completely forgotten, never to return. Violent work is a sure cure for that malady! First, I had to gather the bunt, or centre of the sail, close on top of the middle of the yard, on the fore part of the mast so that I could reach over and under and grasp the short bunt-gasket, pull it over the sail and make it fast on the tie, or halliard, of the yard. Once this was accomplished the real work began. But there was the matter of the foot-ropes. The stirrups were too short so the foot-ropes were too close to the yard, on this yard only. Only at the quarters could one stand comfortably and work, elsewhere it was a matter of crouching and when close to the mast, kneeling on the wire, for here the foot-ropes crossed abaft the mast.

I moved out to the weather side and with my stomach pressed

against the yard, with both hands tried to get a grip on the smooth surface of the canvas. This was not easy. The wind in the half-furled sail forced the material upwards like a rising balloon which strained and flogged itself and me while I fought to create a wrinkle in the fabric which would give me something to grip. An eddy in the wind, probably caused by the movement of the ship far below me, rising, falling and rolling, let the balloon of canvas sag down inert as though in a calm. This was my chance and I quickly gathered the wrinkled folds and tucked them between my stomach and the yard but the false calm lasted only about four seconds. Up shot the ballooning sail and away went the canvas I had gained and the effort had to commence again.

My objective was the foot-rope sewn to the sail. If I could manage to bring that up to the yard and tuck it under my stomach, the wind would be spilled from the sail and there would no longer be a bag which would contain wind. I tried again, and again, and again, but each time that I nearly succeeded a harder gust would gear away my gains and the sail would resume its cursed shape and antics. There were four of these shivering, blasted, perverse, thundering maniacs to be mastered and I attacked them one by one in an elemental fury! Pounding and striking the hard canvas with clenched fists and tearing at it with clawing fingers.

The yard bucked and swayed by the thrashing sail which strained tightly and alternatively flapped furiously while the rolling and pitching of the ship below drew wide invisible arcs and elliptical patterns in the sky. Many times the wind threw the balloon back into my face and high up above me, my hands, forced overhead, had to drop down like lightning to seize the jack-stay, and in doing so I had to turn my hands round so that the palms faced upwards so that my fingers could slide under the jack-stay to grip it, for it was my only hope as my body was forced backwards by the sail. Otherwise I should probably have hit the sea, if I were lucky, or landed on the deck, 160-odd feet below, a mangled piece of pulp. The narrow space between the lower edge of the wood jack-stay and the upper surface of the yard was the only hand-hold up there. Had my fingers encountered the gaps in the jack-stay I might not have lived very long. Luckily my reflexes were excellent. On the other royal yards where the foot-ropes were hung lower it was possible to support oneself by squeezing between the buntlines and leechlines so that they crossed one's back on the lead from the yard to the mast.

Suddenly the sail flapped and collapsed, so grabbing the foot I brought it to the yard, clawing at the rest of the slack canvas. I had won! Passing a few turns of the nearest gasket round yard and sail and hitching it temporarily I moved further inboard gathering the sail's foot as I went. I succeeded in making fast the weather side then crossing over tackled the lee.

Another struggle ensued but not so violent as that which took place on the weather side. Tightening the gaskets to my satisfaction and sliding down the royal backstay I reached the deck, bruised and battered, fingers cramped and stiff, nails broken and chipped while my stomach and chest were red-chafed, but I felt good and had a sense of well-being. I had taken in a sail on my own and I had made a good job of it. I felt proud of my new-found abilities!

As I started to walk forward the Second Mate on the poop whistled through his teeth and signed to me to join him. Mounting the after ladder I approached the officer standing at the weather rail. He gripped my shoulder and nodded aloft.

'You were a long time making fast that royal, boy. It's a bad stow, a very bad stow. Get up there and make a good job of it!'

I listened in deep silence. He gave my shoulder a slight shake.

'All these lumps and bumps, smooth them out and pass the gaskets round the clews.'

He told me how to put a smooth 'skin' of outer canvas over the sail so that as the wind became stronger there would be no cracks or caverns into which its probing fingers would find their way, widening and finally tearing open the furled canvas. The officer concluded his remarks and instruction by saying something about, 'That lot up there—looking like sailor's seabags!'

In the second dog watch we were informed that the Slop Chest was now open. This was an institution peculiar to all deep-water sailing ships, and some tramp steamers, on long voyages. It was simply a retail shop and was usually the per-quisite of the Master, who owned the stock which he bought wholesale and free of duty and sold on credit. Since there was no competition he usually charged what the market would stand, regardless of the shoppers' feelings.

I think that our prices in *Lancing* were fair for there was no growling in the fo'c'sle regarding over-charging. Not much variety was carried on this short voyage for there was only tobacco, soap, safety matches and cocoa, as I recollect. The former was available in cigarette and pipe form, plugs of Fair Maid, Pluck and large tins of some Dutch fine cut. There were also tins of Capstan cigarettes holding 50 and larger tins of the same brand holding flaked tobacco suitable for pipe or cigarette. The roll-your-own brigade used the Dutch and English with very good cigarette papers of French manufacture in double black and gold packets. I tried some of the English tobacco later on, but I would have needed a mustard plaster on the back of my neck to keep it alight. Nevertheless, in later years, as my bellows became more robust, I used it regularly for, as seamen liked it too, it was standard issue in British ships until superseded for some strange reason by Dutch fine cut.

The room had been converted into shop premises by the addition of a portable shelf across the cabin doorway. All hands lined the cabin alleyway again and obtained what they required from the Steward. He had a narrow ledger with a page for each officer and seaman and, behind him, on top of a packing case, were piles of Norwegian Discharge Books. These were pocket-sized paper-backs entitled *Avrengingsbok*, sometimes known as *Kontrabok*. The first page contains the Articles of Agreement. Once a month wages and overtime were entered, personal purchases listed, drawings in port, and advances. There was a new book issued for every ship.

Each time that a seaman attended the Slop Chest, which would be about once every month in fine or moderate weather, he had to produce his book and the cost of his purchases was entered and deducted from his wages at the termination of the voyage. This system has much to recommend it and is, I think, much fairer than the British, for all entries are made under the eyes of the seaman concerned. He can see at any time what his financial standing is and his wages, overtime, fines and so on are not open to abuse.

When it came my turn to be served the Steward seemed

surprised that I should want eight tins of cigarettes and two large tins of Van Houten's cocoa. He demurred at handing out so many cigarettes to such a small boy and I misunderstood his attitude because I thought that all this was an 'issue', a free gift to us from the ship, part of our wages, so I cut my immediate requirements down to four tins of cigarettes and one tin of cocoa. I did not want to be thought greedy, besides I had glimpsed the Chief Mate sitting on a camp stool near the lamp reading a magazine, for it was his cabin.

The new book was handed to me and with this in my hand and the tins inside my shirt I ran forward to the fo'c'sle to open a tin of cigarettes and prepare to smoke myself black in the face. It was here that I found out that I would later be called on to pay for them. The lamp was lit and the accordion was going full blast. The seamen were singing the songs of their, and other, countries while the air grew blue and thickened. One of the Scottish ordinary seamen kept up a staccato rhythm with two big spoons on his knee while another played on a comb wrapped in thin paper. I tried to follow the music with my mouth-organ but I was drowned out by the blasts of the accordion and the feet-stamping and hand-clapping. I gave up and, fetching two six-inch nails from the carpenter's shop, sat in my bunk and used them as drumsticks on the edge of the bunkboard.

All too soon one bell was struck, 1945, and the men due to go on watch from 2000 to midnight began to prepare for it by donning jerseys and warm jackets and the music and singing gradually died away.

Pelle and Larvik prepared for the rigours of the night. They had a length of stiff wire which had been bent to shape and this was now screwed to the end of the bunk to which the lamp was secured, above the after end of the table. The wire formed a stiff and rigid loop which projected over the top of the lamp-glass and about six inches above it. A tin cup holding about a pint of mixed cocoa, sugar and cold water was placed in the loop and left to brew. This usually simmered hot within about three-quarters of an hour but never boiled—luckily for the lamp glass.

No hot water was available during the hours of darkness since the galley was always locked at night. Coffee for the watches was always boiled over a rivet-fire in the donkey boiler-house but this was illegal and was liable to be suspended by authority for any mass breach of discipline.

Larvik and Pelle were generous and allowed others the use of their jury-rig stove and I was offered, on occasion, sips of their cocoa when, as often happened, my own had been exhausted. No man of this very mixed crew was mean with his few possessions. It seemed as though each nationality considered himself a representative of his country and tried to behave accordingly. I have sailed in ships manned by 'townies' (men all from the same port), friends and relatives (not mine) and men drawn from the same district or parish, but always I have found that a mixture of nationalities brings out the best in a crew. They may slightly despise each other's national publicized characteristics but seamen as a rule have a very broad and tolerant outlook.

The eight, sharp, double clangs of the big bell and the mournful long-drawn-out cry of 'All-l-l-l-s wel-l-l-l-l' of the look-out man above us, put an abrupt end to the festivities and activity within the deck-house as we hurried aft to muster at the poop.

I liked the sound of the cry of the look-out man, it was so in keeping with the character of the ship and the waste of waters which surrounded us. It was an eerie, lonely cry but very reassuring, especially when the weather was wild. The voice slowly rising on the 'all', gradually dropping on the 'well' and tapering off to silence.

In the steamers in which I later served the recognized cry was '*Lights* are *bright* and all's well, sir!' delivered in a rapid conversational shout which conveyed nothing more to the listener than that the side-lights and mast-head lights were burning and that the look-out man was awake. Many times this garbled shout was caught by the wind and was too brief to be audible on the bridge. I never mentioned lights when calling, since it was assumed that they were burning brightly. But if one shouted out something about lights, then was the time for the officer to investigate. There is very little difference between 'Lights are bright, sir!' and 'Lights are out, sir!' when called out in a rising wind to a Mate who is 'miles away' in a corner of the bridge wing, or busy in the chartroom.

So, during all my seafaring I ignored the lights-are-bright

routine and continued the call of 'all's well'. A fireman in one tramp steamer said to me, 'Christ, Jock, it gives yer the creeps but it's good to know yer up there, ye *sound* like a sailor!' I took this in a complimentary sense, hoping that it was not a reflection on my ability as a seaman. Another piece of advice which I followed throughout the period during which I served before the mast was the deliberate dropping of the word 'sir'. As Blackbeard advised,

'Don't use the word *sir*, when you have to repeat an order given to you by an officer. And don't use it either when you report the conditions while on look-out. It's a waste of time and breath and it could be confusing. At all other times, yes, give the officer the respect due to him.' He further explained,

'When given a direct order it is an unbreakable rule that you must repeat that order *exactly* word for word as it is given to you, so that the officer knows that you have heard it all right and will act upon it. The officer will not say to the seaman who is steering the ship, "Down a bit—bring her up half a point, *sir*!" Now will he? So, strictly speaking, you are violating an iron-clad rule when you tack on the word *sir* to the repeat of an order.'

During my voyage in *Lancing* a number of my cherished beliefs were shattered, particularly this nonsense about one hand for the ship—and one for yourself! I had read of this saying in books and had even heard it from the lips of seamen who should have known better but when I came to put it into practice while working aloft or over the side, I quickly found it to be a myth.

No man can work efficiently under sailing ship conditions with only one hand while he hangs on with the other. A seaman uses balance to perform his work. From the moment that a ship sails until she docks again the seaman is balancing, even in his bunk and the camber of the decks of a motionless vessel ensure that he is never truly perpendicular to whatever he is standing on. The seaman leans. He leans against ropes which are taut, against the masts, the yards, the standing rigging, and even the wind! He can slide down a dangling rope, twist one leg around it, put the sole of one foot on top of the toes of the other with the loose rope between, and work in comparative comfort with both hands. A good active seaman is an unindentured acrobat and whoever invented the myth about 'one-handed work' must have been a claims adjuster.

I met another insurance-safety-first fiddle later when I joined a four-masted barque. My first time aloft in her I found that she had large wire grommets seized to the jack-stays and spaced about six feet apart. I asked an apprentice near by what were they intended to be used for. He said they were for 'holding on to when we take in sail!' Of course nobody ever used them except as a lead for the gasket when making fast the courses.

There was none of this exaggerated impractical safety-first and netting-under-the bowsprit nonsense aboard *Lancing*. When an emergency arose it was tackled quickly and sensibly. One day, with the ship thrashing through the seas, close-hauled on the port tack, it was seen that the shackle pin of the lee main clew garnet had lost its mousing, worked loose and buried itself in the ocean and the whip was swinging to leeward, the tackle now useless for raising the heavy sail to the yard when required. The wind was strong and, rather than slack off the sheet and goosewing the sail by other and more laborious methods, the Second Mate decided to effect a quick repair.

A line was passed round both parts of the main sheet close to the sheave in the bulwark and the end brought back inboard and this bight brought forward along the straining sheet, as near to the clew as possible. All the watch tailed on and hove away but the combined effort only succeeded in gaining about half a fathom. A heavy tackle would be required to bring the straining clew close to the t'gallant rail. Pelle had a few quick words with the Second Mate and from the exclamations in English and gestures of some of the men I understood what was afoot and climbed into the rigging, mounting about five ratlines and calling out that I could reach it!

Only two of the men looked up and one gave me a sour look. I was completely ignored. I was desperately anxious to jump into the curves of the clew, not simply to show off but because it was an opportunity to do something that I considered I was fit to perform by nature. I was small, light in weight, the wind was in my favour and the gap to be crossed was only about two fathoms. My mind did not go beyond these facts.

Pelle thrust an iron shackle into a hip pocket together with a small coiled length of seizing wire. He did not require to shed any garment for, as usual, he wore no jacket or shirt, just a striped singlet open to the navel, for he was a hard case who only wore a shirt in real bad weather. (Later, I sailed with his double, an Englishman named Cock Sanderson.) Pelle climbed up alongside me and standing on a lower ratline measured the distance carefully, waiting for a steeper roll to leeward, then he crouched and jumped outboard, landing against the big sail in a standing position his bare feet scrabbling for a toe-hold on the canvas, his hands fastened to the swaying leech. His body moved away from the security of the sail and he was etched against the sea but his feet had found anchorage as his toes fastened on the clew iron. He swayed back and waited for the clew-garnet whip to swing within reach but a seaman had gone aloft, and, lifting the tackle, dropped the block down against the sail within reach of Pelle, who now straddled the big sheet block, his legs twisted through the two parts of the sheet as he shackled the clew-garnet block to the ring of the spectacle. A marline-spike was thrown to him with which he tightened the shackle pin, then putting on a wire mousing to complete the job he slowly climbed up the now-taut clew-garnet, the marline-spike hanging down his back from the lanyard round his neck. The bowsing lashing round the main sheet was cast off and the watch dispersed.

'Aye . . .' said one of the able seamen to me afterwards, '. . . but ye wouldn't know what the hell to do when ye got out there!' I recognized the truth when I heard it, for that is the way to learn. Watch better men.

CHAPTER EIGHT

Heavy Weather and Hard Work

During the next few days nothing much happened of note except that I received another bashing from the young Finn. I do not remember now exactly what it was that caused him to start on me but it had something to do with scrubbing out the fo'c'sle on Saturday morning.

Three or four boys and ordinary seamen usually performed this task together and within an hour the job was completed. We cleared everything out except the bogey stove. This useful and comforting piece of iron furniture was dismantled later and stowed down the forepeak for it used precious coal. The two benches were taken out on deck and scrubbed while the seachests were stowed under the fo'c'sle-head then replaced and lashed in their correct positions when the job had been completed. The table was raised up to the deck-head, sliding on its two supporting stanchions, and wedged there, clear of all heads.

I have an idea that, as we sloshed the sea-water around, one of us, probably me, splashed the Finn as he lay sleeping in the bunk under Pelle's, for I remember him jumping out of his bunk and sailing into me with his fists. I did not attempt to retaliate but I was prepared to defend myself without striking back for to do so would, I was sure, result in real violence and maybe bloodshed. I covered-up, ducked and dodged, managed accidentally to kick a broom and roll a bucket against his bare feet, then fled to the deck, where I stood near the fore part of the windlass surrounded by seachests and watched warily as he mouthed his native curses and threats at me from within the fo'c'sle. The broom and bucket came flying through the doorway but I let them lie where they landed while I went out on deck and joined my watch. The other youths finished the job without my assistance.

We were about ten days out from Ardrossan when I came within a 'midge's whisker' of losing my life. I go cold even now when I think of it. I had noticed an absence of seagulls those last few days, since none came for the scraps I dumped overboard. I mentioned this to one of the seamen.

'Hell, yu' never see them bastards at sea, there's no grub for them out here. They always hang around the land.' From this he passed to observations about the weather, and looking at the lowering heavy clouds and listening to the song of the hardening wind, he forecast. 'Dirty, bloody weather comin' our way. We'll be handin' them big courses soon.' He meant that we would be taking in the mainsail and the mizzen, the largest sails in the ship. Other experienced seamen voiced the same thought.

Sure enough, before another hour had passed both watches were hauling away at clew-garnets and buntlines as the big mizzen bellied up around both parts of the mizzen stay when the sheets and the tack were slacked off. It thrubbed, thrubbed, flapped wetly, cracked and thundered while the clew-irons added the harsh ring of metal to the din. Our voices mixed with the wind and the rattling-clacking of patent block sheaves as we sang and howled,

'Ah waa-aaa-huh! Oh Ranzo! A waaay hayyy-hey! Lift yer skirts up, girlie! Oh way-hey-ho-ha! Aye-e-e-e-e!' A shouted order, 'Belay that—belay all!'

The ship was sailing fast, heeling well over to starboard. She had an easy motion and rolled to windward slightly before heeling steeply to leeward. The seas on the lee beam were wind-whipped white with the fog of driven spume, while the horizon lifted high above the t'gallant rail and slowly sank down—irregularly. The crash, whisper and hissing of creaming, tumbling seas alongside blended with the thundering of the sail and the shouts and cries of officers and men working to subdue a giant before it split asunder and was gone! It was here that I learned to collect and use my senses in the midst of such pandemonium.

Came the final hoarse yell of the old Chief Mate, 'Aloft an' furl!' and we all took to the rigging, including the Second Mate and the Cook! The Captain was on the poop while the old Mate stayed below on the main deck to slack or take in on any lines we called for.

I found myself at the bunt, beside the Cook and the Second Mate while the bight of the weather leech was fought with, then passed along the yard, then the foot followed by the canvas which was thumped and banged with fists until all the lumps had been hammered out flat and the gaskets passed to secure it. Then we all moved over to the lee side. This move put me well out towards the yard-arm but even so the foot-rope was too low for me. A sailor of the port watch, next to me shouted, 'Get down on the foot-rope, Yack.' I did not understand what he wanted me to do. 'Sit on the foot-rope and pass the gasket up to me,' he cried, looking back down at me. I was amazed. *Sit* on a single wire under the yard, 40 feet above the deck— what was I going to hang on to? There was no supporting stirrup wire near me for I was right in the centre of the catenary of the wire; however, trusting my elders I lowered myself down until I was sitting on the wire with my forehead pressed against the cold iron of the big yard. I used my head to retain my balance while the weight of my legs and feet gave me a kind of ballast keel suspended below the wire. With both hands free I coiled the swinging gasket and flipped it up on the fore side of the yard to the stretching, grasping fingers of the seaman.

I had not been warned about what was to happen next and I had not foreseen it. The sail had been gathered to the yard but now it had to be rolled on top of the spar and this operation called for a concerted effort by all hands working together. The Second Mate called out something which I did not understand, then gave a long drawn-out hauling cry ending with a savage, 'Wayyy-Hey!' Every man standing on the footrope braced himself, leaned far out and with the cry of 'Hey' heaved backwards with the sail. As they had all leaned far forward the foot-rope had lifted to a nearly horizontal position with the yard and I had nothing to grasp. I was sitting upright on a wire in half a gale of wind, at least three feet abaft the yard, forced away from comparative safety by the power of 46 straining legs. I had been totally unprepared for this sudden alteration in altitude and my guts performed a dance while one hand shot out towards the yard which I just touched with the tips of my fingers only. My other hand holding the gasket was useless. Luckily my head which had been pressing the cold iron had shot upright as the wire moved, so that and the balanced weight of my legs and the tips of my fingers were all that saved me from a rapid descent to the deck.

Just as suddenly the foot-rope sagged down into place as the sail was hove on to the yard. The hard force of the wind on my back must have aided me to retain balance. I hastened to wriggle along the wire until I was beside the seaman who had given me that suicidal instruction. I was safe now because each time that the foot-rope rose into the air I hung on to the top of his seaboot or his belt. I was never caught in the centre of a sagging foot-rope again. I made sure there was a stirrup or a pair of legs handy.

We took in the mainsail after this—and lost some sleep. Since both watches had been engaged in the operation it had been timed to commence an hour before the change of watches and it had lasted two hours, so each watch lost one hour's rest.

Spray was flying across the decks in solid sheets as the big ship drove through the seas and every man, but one, now wore oilskin suits as a matter of course. I was the odd man out since the mistake which I had made in Sinclar's shop in Ardrossan was costing me dearly now. I had chosen an oilskin coat in preference to a suit of trousers and jacket because I had seen the Mates wearing them during rain showers in Glasgow.

An oilskin coat is a menace to a seaman in a windjammer. It pins one to the rigging and the skirt wraps itself round the backstay one happens to be sliding down and it tears. On a yard aloft, the wind gets inside it and it blows over one's head like an umbrella turned turtle and, for that reason, it can be extremely dangerous. It cannot keep one dry on deck because the seas simply rise up under it and fill one's seaboots too.

When I entered the fo'c'sle during the dog-watch, dripping wet and with my new oilskin torn across the sleeve and the bottom, the seamen took pity on my bedraggled state and rooted around for old oilskin suits which I could wear. I was grateful to them for their kindness for they went to some trouble to fit me out. Old and tattered oilskin pants and jackets were unearthed from seachests and when opened out from their mummified state, the act of tearing the folds apart reminded me of a plaster ripped from a hairy skin.

'Cast-offs' hanging on wood pegs near the port door were spread over the table or held up to the light of the lamp before being draped on me. An argument developed and became a trifle heated when one young seaman said that if the bottoms of a pair of pants were cut off, they would fit me fine. An older seaman laughed at this and pointed out that it was the top part that required shortening otherwise the crotch would be down around my knees and I would never be able to climb aloft. Even the music stopped while the points were demonstrated and I was shoved around and made to stand on the bench.

Finally a cast-off which some 'parish-rigged' sailor had converted from a boiler-suit overall, in a fit of desperation or sheer genius, was minutely examined, its shortcomings discussed and analysed, was cut to size and presented to me. It had worn soft and rubbery and had a pattern of thousands of small cracks running across each other. The fastenings were spring clips such as were common on American overalls and oilskin coats at one time and, of course, it opened from the neck to the crotch so for that reason alone it was far from watertight. However, I wore the thing for a week or two even though it leaked and I was always damp inside it, but it was better than being perpetually drenched. With 'soul and body lashings' round my wrists and seaboots I was reasonably dry in bad weather. It was ultimately discarded for a real old suit, cut to fit and donated by, I think, the Sailmaker.

During the night we took in the four royals and two boys were assigned to each as the wind was strong and was accompanied by squalls and heavy rain. The air was cold, too. Later, when I came on watch again at about midnight, two seamen and I were ordered to stand-by the main upper t'gallant halliards. I remember one of the seamen distinctly.

He was a big man, a slow, silent but friendly man and he had, to my mind, the appearance of a scholar, though he was not. I thought of him as the Schoolmaster. He was over six feet in height with a lumpy body. His face was pale for a seaman and his cheeks sagged slightly either side of his mouth. He was clean shaven and his head was completely bald on top but with funny little silvery tufts of hair above each ear. He often went bare-headed in the worst of weather yet he wore a blue woollen stocking cap when not on watch or sitting up in his bunk.

When about to prepare for sleep he would remove the cap,

roll it up and tuck it under his pillow of shirts and coats, then with a circular motion he would massage his head, take off his steel-rimmed spectacles used for reading and put them carefully on the shelf. He nearly always went to sleep lying flat on his back, like a hospital patient, with the blanket drawn up to his chin and his big hands resting lifelessly at his hips, over the blanket. He spoke very good English in slow quiet tones and I think now that he was a Britisher.

The hauling part of the halliard was led to a hand winch situated on top of the midship house on the starboard side, close to the donkey boiler casing. There was a protective rail of iron stanchions and chains along a short length of the deckhouse top beside this winch. Eight bells had struck, we mustered aft and were ordered to relieve the men of the port watch who were standing by the halliards ready to let go when the expected emergency of a screaming wind squall arose. As usual I was late turning out. I always managed to muster with the rest of my watch but I had not had time to don sufficient clothing suitable to the weather. This did not worry me because I thought that I could nip back into the fo'c'sle as I had managed to do on other occasions, but this time I could not. I had not reckoned on a job of work!

We three stood at the winch on the top of the deck-house, fully exposed to the cold, cutting wind and whipping spray for what, to me, seemed hours. I was shivering and trembling with cold, my jaws were locked to prevent my teeth hammering like driven rivets and, though I thumped my arms across my chest and knocked my feet together one by one as I crouched, I was just an animated icicle. The Schoolmaster showed pity after about half-an-hour, and said, with his face close to my blue features, 'Get down on the deck an' stand-by in the lee of the house, we'll call you up here if we need you.' Thankfully I climbed down the ladder fixed to the side of the house abaft the mainmast, and moved stiffly round to the lee where I continued my vigil. I was mighty glad to be off the top of that house for here in the lee I was sheltered from the wind and though soaking wet I felt, by comparison, a certain warmth. I thought of my towel hanging beside my bunk, of my dry clothes in the seachest, of my parish-rig oilskin swaying on a peg, all less than 50 feet distant.

We were kept standing-by for over an hour as the squalls, following one behind another, swept over the flying, rushing ship. I watched the seas beyond the lee rail rear up as she heeled to a squall. They appeared in the darkness to be about to climb over the high bulwarks as the breaking crests foamed white and luminous and thrashed each other wildly then sank out of sight as the ship rolled back gently to windward. I shall never forget that cold, cold period as I stood swaying on the iron deck and suffered the punishment of laziness. Finally a shout dismissed us and the halliards were not started.

A cold, sharp daylight brought no change in the weather. To look out on the sea was to gaze on desolation. Cold, grey, wind-whipped waters and flying spray from breaking crests left puddles of foam behind them in the troughs. A faint whistle from aft brought Larvik the look-out man down from the fo'c'sle-head with the port sidelight while Pelle went up and brought the other down to the lamp locker, unasked. Larvik reported later, 'Second says she is doing 16 knots!'

The figures of Captain Pedersen and the Second Mate, Mr Hansen, were visible on the poop. They were standing near the wheel-house trunk dressed in oilskin long coats. We were standing by under the shelter of the fo'c'sle-head smoking and looking aft, watching the stern of the ship rising and falling on the run of the seas. A voice, 'Won't be long now. Old Man's lookin' aloft!' A chorus of grunting assent followed the speaker's observation. We were expecting to have to take in the t'gallant sails and were hoping that we would have time to swallow our six o'clock coffee before starting to clew up the sails.

The Second Mate left the Captain's side and walked forward towards the poop ladder, his body held at a steep angle to counteract the slope of the deck. 'Here we go!' a voice exclaimed in fateful resignation and our watch stirred and moved as one man, following the lead of the Bo'sun's Mate out to the open main deck. As we did so, three blasts of a whistle were driven towards us on the rising gale.

We clewed up and furled the jigger upper t'gallant sail, battling and cursing the hard, wet canvas while the other half of the watch were taking in the fore upper t'gallant sail. The faint notes of four bells sounded as we finished our work aloft and I longed for my pint of hot, sweet, black coffee as I descended the weather rigging. The wind was too strong for me to chance sliding down a backstay.

As we swung down off the main rail the Second Mate was waiting.

'All right, mizzen upper t'gallant sail next!'

A seaman spoke loudly, 'Christ, no coffee?' The Second Mate affected not to have heard the remark and moved towards the mizzen t'gallant halliards.

Another seaman called after him, 'What's all the rush, Mister? They've stood all night—another ten minutes won't make no difference!'

The officer could no longer ignore the speakers. He swung round on one man and pushing his face close to that of the seaman, stamped one foot on the deck and cursed him in Norwegian while his voice rose and his face grew redder and redder! I saw that his hands were clenched into trembling fists and I knew then that Mr Hansen had a temper.

We thought there was going to be a fight, for it was not uncommon for officers to mix it with seamen in windjammers but Mr Hansen controlled himself just long enough. The Bo'sun's Mate turned back and in sharp tones ordered us to the clewlines and buntlines. The seamen shrugged shoulders and with a muttered curse moved away while the officer turned on his heel and made for the halliards. As he slacked away we hauled on the lines while the Bo'sun's Mate and the cause of the trouble manned the downhauls.

We drank our coffee an hour later, outside the galley, and watched the Captain's son bring the dog on a lead out on to the main deck for its morning unloading in the scuppers. This day was a Sunday and we looked forward to a brief respite from the usual work of the ship but according to the seamen, who were wise in the weather, we would not get much rest that week-end!

The turns of look-out became more frequent as there were now two men required at the wheel. Ed, the ex-apprentice, had distinguished himself early in the voyage by nearly putting the ship aback during his first trick at the wheel the day after we left port so he had, I think, been disrated to ordinary seaman and was only permitted to take a 'lee wheel' when necessary. This was to enable him to learn how to steer a sailing ship and help him to regain his rating, and rate of pay when fully qualified. Fortunately the weather was fairly mild at the time or we would all have been in trouble. He cursed and swore and advanced various excuses on his return to the fo'c'sle, disgraced. He received no sympathy. One young able seaman gave him a right cursing and told him what he thought of his 'flamin' bloody cheek' signing on a ship 'when ye can't do a boy's job properly, let alone a man's. Gettin' money under false pretences!' There was a deep chorus of agreement when it was pointed out that the seamen would have to do *his* wheel now. Ed, of course, knew what to do in this situation. He removed his jacket, dropped his braces, grabbed some paper and disappeared in the direction of the lavatory.

After a breakfast of burgoo, egg and salt bacon, with coffee, we turned in but most of the experienced seamen kept their trousers on and their seaboots handy for, they said, 'The Old Man, he won't carry this sail much longer. It's blowin' a full gale. Be "all hands shorten down" soon—you see!'

We had just time to be comfortable and drowsy in our bunks before someone drew our attention to the three blasts of the whistle and the Sailmaker clad in dripping oilskins entered the fo'c'sle and announced happily, 'All hands on deck—shorten sail—lively now!' No sooner had he departed than the Second Mate came to the lee doorway and told us that we were about to 'wear ship' and to get aft to the weather cro'jack brace. One of the seamen groaned, 'It *would* come on a Sunday!'

We hurriedly dressed in seaboots and oilskins and rigged our 'Soul-and-body' lashings as we staggered aft along the streaming decks which heeled over sharply to starboard. We were given an amused welcome as we passed the port watch standing ready at the weather braces. We gathered at the mizzen fife-rail and found that the coils of the jigger braces had been prepared for us by the men of the other watch.

The wind was strong and cold with a rising sea and the next hour or so was a period of hauling and sweating as the yards were slowly squared while the helm was put up and the ship run off before the wind. This action brought her upright and the roar of the wind in the rigging diminished while the vessel rolled and pitched gracefully.

The stern rose up on the crest of a big, breaking sea which

foamed and hissed behind us as the bows went down. There came a pause, then the bowsprit was flung skyward and another great sea rose up in awesome majesty and appeared for a brief moment to be about to crash aboard over the counter, but at the critical moment the stern rose and the breaking crest dropped out of sight to reappear later a hundred feet astern with the trailing log-line coasting down into the trough.

The speed had increased as the ship had been run off and now *Lancing* was knifing through the seas like a cruiser on trials. The spume pattern of the crushed and broken bow waves swam heaving past her flying sides in jumbled confusion. Her speed at this time was discussed later in the fo'c'sle and according to what the helmsmen had overheard while at the wheel it was 13 knots. Apparently this was not unusual for her, for she had been known to log 20 knots in favourable conditions and keep it up for a considerable time, until the seas became too dangerous and sail had to be taken in.

As the ship was brought up to the wind again on the other tack, the scream of the gale increased once more and the vessel listed over on her port side while her speed dropped. Seas now broke against the weather bow and the spray was flung high above the rail to be caught by the wind, flattened and whipped across the deck in stinging sheets.

The Sailmaker had been right. Our next job was to take in sail. Hour after hour we toiled, clewing up the four t'gallant sails and climbing aloft to furl and stow them. Our watch took the mizzen and jigger masts while the port watch performed on the fore and main. Custom decrees that the forward half of a ship is usually worked by the Chief Mate while the after half is the responsibility of the Second Mate. There are no hard and fast rules about this but this is what usually occurs when all hands are working together, such as when entering and leaving port.

We returned to the deck with empty stomachs and thoughts of dinner, but it was not to be. Midday came and passed with both watches spread out along the fore upper topsail yard. When that had been made fast we trooped aft to clew up and furl the jigger upper topsail. The ship was now snugged down to the fore topmast staysail, foresail and lower topsail, both topsails on the main and two on the mizzen with a lower topsail

1. Four-masted ship, *Lancing*.

2. *Lancing's* stern with propeller aperture sealed. Built as an iron screw steamer, she was later converted and as a sailing ship proved herself a real flier.

Photos: Donald B. MacCulloch.

3. Bow view of *Lancing* in Govan dry dock, December 1920.

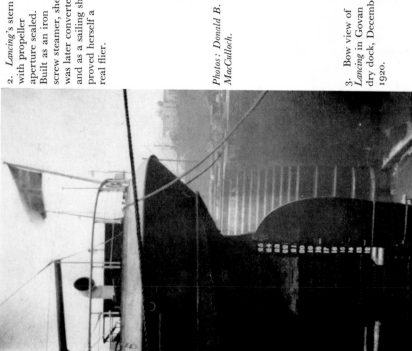

on the jigger. Three lower staysails completed her sail area and, according to reliable information, she was still travelling at a speed of nine knots, close-hauled in a north-west wind of force 9–10.

This is what brought many seamen to her like a magnet. They would go out of their way to sign in her, even though they knew in advance that she was a 'back-breaking workhouse'. They simply wanted to boast in other fo'c'sles that 'I sailed in *Lancing!*' She stamped their Discharge Books with the pride of her achievements as the sailer of sailing ships, the fastest of her kind. And by her historical uniqueness she gave them also many, many long hours of conversational interest.

Mostly it was the Scandinavian people who felt this pride in her, if not by direct association then by historical reports. But we others were drawn in and gradually, because merchant seamen have an absorbing interest in a great ship and an international outlook which disregards national flags when the subject which wears them excites their curiosity and engenders their admiration; we held our heads a little higher when in the company of fellow seamen.

We had our dinner at last, standing around the table, sitting on the lashed benches with backs pressed against it and a supporting foot on the top of a seachest opposite, or wedged into a bunk with bowl or plate in one hand and a single tool in the other, holding on to anything as we moved about.

The day wore on with the seas increasing in size and the decision was made to heave-to. So off we went again. We clewed-up and made fast the big foresail, then main and mizzen upper topsails, ran down and stowed in the nettings the fore and main staysails and braced the yards hard up. Then all hands were ordered off the deck. Some went up on the poop, others, like myself, into the mizzen rigging. At the right moment the helm was put down and the ship brought up to the wind, hove-to on the starboard tack.

The ship was now lying-to, stopped to all intents and purposes, head-reaching a little, falling off, then coming up to the wind again, drifting. The seas were tearing towards our starboard bow, their white crests rearing higher as they neared the ship and appearing ready to engulf her, but the bows would rise swiftly and the wave would break against the plating at the

G

waterline and appear to pass below the forefoot only to re-appear on the port bow, smooth and growling, travelling swiftly and harmlessly south.

Darkness, as it always does, brought an ominous and eerie note to the storm. Its effect was to frighten us, to make us cower, to induce us to believe that conditions were now much worse than when we had seen them an hour ago; that the seas were mounting and the wind was rising and that danger was fast approaching and death lurked for every man beyond the t'gallant rail. I saw anxiety in more than one pair of eyes that night, as the ship rolled, staggered and paused over-long before rolling back.

Now that the ship, practically denuded of canvas, had lost her forward motion and the wind no longer had a large expanse of sail to push against, it howled and screamed through the harp-strings of the bare rigging, sometimes moaning softly as the vessel lurched swiftly to leeward and rising to a shrieking crescendo as she threw her masts back up to windward. The two parts of the doubled fore and main topmast stays, having no sails now set on them, chattered like sewing machines, adding their unfamiliar noise to the insidious quiet panic that the darkness was trying to instil in us.

I had a look-out during the night and we were instructed to remain on top of the deck-house and not to go on to the fo'c'sle-head in case a sea swept over it. I think it must have been the Bo'sun who issued that precautionary order and not an officer, because the fo'c'sle-head was the driest part of the ship when I was on the look-out.

However, I obeyed the order and stayed on the deck-house though it was an uncomfortable place to be. One did not have sufficient room to sway one's body in a complete circle in opposition to the movements of the ship, for the big longboat and the pram dinghy, both stowed bottom up, occupied most of the available space and one could not move about for fear of disturbing the sleep of the watch below. So I contented myself by standing abaft the steam winch, leaning against the fork of the mainstay and watching with fascination the elemental fury of the storm.

Sometimes, when a line of white combers reared up higher than the rest and approached the starboard bow with a noise like thunder, seeming about to sweep across the deck, I would scramble hurriedly aft on the lee side of the dinghy, hold on and turn to watch destruction. But it never happened. The breaking wave would sink down as it reached the bowsprit guys and with a heave and a wide roll to leeward the ship would slide down its back. I felt the cold and feverish fear of the night but I had great and trusting faith in the seamanship of Captain Pedersen and the Mates and in the abilities of the majority of the able seamen, so I was never unduly worried. I did not possess the experience to know what could happen to a sailing ship and her crew under various circumstances. But I was learning rapidly.

My next look-out was kept on the fo'c'sle-head in daylight and at the height of the storm. I saw then what I had missed seeing in the darkness. The colours and the shadows and the sheer, breath-taking majesty and threatening brutality of the power of the sea, its wild, free, primeval beauty. For two enchanted hours I stood there in the bows, close to the knight-heads and drank in this wild and lovely scene, swaying loose-kneed against the plunging, rolling vessel and staggering often as the wind tore and buffeted me.

I sang aloud for I knew that no one aboard could hear me above the screaming and howling of the wind through the rigging. I had no words to put to the songs for I had been too lazy to learn them. But I matched my puny voice to the notes of the storm with extracts from operas and *Songs Without Words*, Mendelssohn's *Hebrides* and *Träumerei*, and *Scots-wa-hae* with long drawn-out notes in every key I could manage, giving a complete range of sounds to accompany the voice of the gale. I was exhilarated, glad beyond words to be where I was, and I knew I had found happiness. *This* was what I had been seeking.

The wind had torn the curtain of cloud from the sky and the weak sunlight heightened the creamy, bubbling whites, the deep and beckoning blues, purples and emeralds of the sea and formed behind my eyes an unforgettable and unsurpassed scene of glory. The bows plunged down, down, down, until it seemed that the ship was about to be engulfed by the wild sea which reared up to meet them, roaring, fuming and coldly boiling, then as the bows dipped deep into the waters they suddenly slowed in their descent, obeying their inbuilt buoyancy and stopped when the turmoiled surface of the sea was licking and frothing at the shackles of the bowsprit guys. There was an imperceptible pause then the bows flung up high into the air and free of the sea and instead of the horizon being a mere 50 feet in front of my eyes it now was many, many waves away. I could see far over the storm-wracked waters and count wave after wave stretching far into the windy distance, the trailing lines of torn spume lying inert and writhing in the troughs from crest to crest. Then again the bows would pause at the limit of their reach and slowly then swiftly commence the downward plunge, and the movements be repeated time after time— endlessly.

As the bows swiftly sank my weight would lessen and I had the sensation of being as light as an empty seabag but as they reared up to the sky again my weight returned threefold and I felt as though my feet were being forced down through the wooden deck planking.

Turning I looked at the bare, stripped yards behind me, so strange and unfamiliar now. Watching the gyrations of the masts swinging violently but gracefully across the arc of the sky, I marvelled that I had managed to remain aloft for two minutes, let alone climb about and work up there for hours. It appeared impossible that men could be really comfortable and at home while moving about on these wildly swinging metal tubes, standing on a single wire and, at times, holding on to nothing more substantial than a wisp of wind.

The gale lasted about 30 or 40 hours and during the period while the ship was hove-to, the decks were comparatively dry while the sun appeared intermittently. There was some rainfall but it was slight. Finally, as the storm moderated, the ship was put back on her course, sail was made and the area was gradually increased until she was once more sailing towards the sunset, across the Western Ocean.

CHAPTER NINE

Never Sleep on Watch!

By Tuesday the gale had dropped to the strength of a strong wind and the following day the ship was sailing through moderate seas under all sail. We were back to normal again and I was, with two other boys, lent to the Sailmaker who was opening out some sails for repair.

I enjoyed this work which I found interesting but exhausting. The sails were heavy and, to add to the weight of the canvas, there was the stiff wire roping sewn to the foot and leeches, the manila bolt-rope sewn to the head, the hardwood bullseyes, and galvanized metal cringles roped to the leeches. Then every single eyelet along the head and the reef-band had a galvanized metal ring concealed by stitching. The big heavy galvanized iron clew spectacles, or clew irons, to which the sheet, tack and clewline would be attached were, I noticed, of similar pattern to the tiny hooks-and-eyes which my mother and sisters sewed to their various garments as fasteners, before the days of the universal zipper.

Because of the sheer weight and size of the sails and so that they could be moved about they were made up, or folded, in a different fashion to the method adopted with a hatch tarpaulin which is made up square, for they were folded along their width, which was their greatest length, the folds taking a zig-zag form with the final fold being used as a 'skin' over all.

The completed sail formed a long, cylindrical bundle with many lumps due to the folded wire-roping and bullseyes. At each end of the cylinder the clew irons and the head earing cringle were left free. A seaman straddled a portion of the sail, lifted it and held it by the inward pressure of his knees, leaving his hands free to pass a rope-yarn lashing round the supported portion, tying one lashing every four feet or so. Each lashing was put on exactly over the sailcloth seams as that was the strongest and thickest part, less liable to chafe with the movement of the ship while in the locker.

The object in making up the sails in this manner was to enable them to be moved entirely by man-power, to pass through narrow hatchways and to be bent to the yards in heavy weather, without being opened out fully, as replacements for damaged or blown-away sails.

The remains of a sail could be sent down from aloft on the end of a mast-head gantline and the new sail brought out of the sail locker and hoisted aloft (exactly as it was stowed away) and stretched along the yard, the head earing passed and the clew garnet, or line shackled on, buntlines, leech-lines rove off and the sail bent to the yard by rope-yarn ties, called 'robands' or 'rovings', then the sail set, or made fast in the gaskets. At least that was the theory, but it was a long and arduous job for the seamen and mates in a big, short-handed vessel such as *Lancing*.

A sail was always marked with the initials of its name stencilled across the clew, between the leech and the foot. When made up canvas labels roughly marked with black paint and bearing the same initials were seized to the clew spectacles, or irons. When stowed in the sail locker all the clews of every sail were brought to the outside of each tier for instant identification and when found and hoisted to the deck, the label was removed and hung with others in the locker. If the sail was inscribed 'MA-UT' it was the main upper topsail. If marked 'XJ' or merely a *cross*, it was the cro'jack, and so on. These initials are English, not Norwegian.

When a large sail had to be moved about the decks it was a matter for all the watch (and probably the Cook) to hoist it on their shoulders and walk away with it. To get this 90-foot by 20-inch diameter sausage on to our shoulders was fairly easy. We had only to stand alongside it and three or four men picked up a bight and dumped it on one. They then moved along giving a repeat performance to the other men after which they themselves got under the sagging lengths and we all staggered away with it.

I sometimes found myself carrying nothing because I happened to be between two others taller than myself. When that was discovered I was chased away to the end which was heavier because it had the clew irons spliced into it and they battered the backs of one's legs and ankles as they swung with the movement.

Canvas plays havoc with one's finger-nails and mine were always broken and chipped. My hands I noticed were hardening properly, no thanks to the previous advice given by the seasoned sailors—with the exception of Blackbeard, of course. I had had my baptism of salt since everything I touched on deck or aloft was sticky with it, until the rains came. My hands were in danger of becoming pickled, however I was satisfied with the hard lumps of skin which had replaced the blisters and I was conscious that my fingers no longer hung straight down from my hands but curved inwards when at rest, like the fingers of the experienced seamen whose years of climbing, gripping and hauling on ropes and lines had given them this ape-like contortion.

* * *

One quiet night I stepped straight into a real picture and became a living part of an advertisement for passenger travel by sea!

It was a calm night, with little wind and a silver moon, away to the south-west, cast a path of shimmering radiance across the ruffled sea and bathed our sails and decks with soft brilliance and deep moving shadows.

Lancing was sailing close-hauled on the starboard tack with all canvas set and drawing, making about five knots through the water. The night was so quiet that the footfalls of the seamen on deck were clearly audible. The Look-outman on the fo'c'sle-head pacing slowly athwartships was easily identified. The time was about 2230 and the Captain had just gone below to the cabin leaving the Second Mate in charge of the deck. I knew that a steamer was approaching for I had heard our bell reporting and seen her lights earlier, about three points off the lee bow.

I was alone and performing some simple task aft, coiling lines on the pins at the weather jigger rigging when I saw Mr Hansen descend the after poop ladder and enter the wheelhouse. A match was ignited and illuminated the doorway for a brief instant then was extinguished with a click of metal. The

Second Mate emerged carrying a brass signalling lamp which had a sliding shutter worked by a thumb key. It was a paraffin lamp of the bullseye type, measuring about ten inches in height with a diameter of about four or five inches with a handle on the left side, the key being on the right. He returned to the poop carrying the lamp from which no light escaped until the key was depressed and the shutter flicked open.

Completing my work and mounting the ladder to the poop I stood near the wheel-house trunk, out of the way of the officer, who, facing the approaching steamer, rested the lamp on the white-painted port rail and glancing aloft and round his own decks first, waited for the big vessel to draw nearer.

When she was within a mile or so of us and approaching our lee bow, she altered course about three points to starboard and I saw her mast-head lights, one above the other, draw apart. The act of altering course exposed her port side to our view and I saw line above line of lighted ports and brilliant electric lighting along her open decks. She was a big passenger liner of about 20,000 tons with four masts and two light-coloured funnels with black tops.

She drew very close and, although she was silhouetted against the moon, the reflected light from the sea enabled me to distinguish every detail of her. I listened to the rhythmic, thundering pounding of her steam engines and the fainter music of an orchestra playing a waltz. The Second Mate had called her up with the lamp as she approached and the clicking sound of the key, his body outlined against the bright halo of the flashing light, together with the answering winking flashes from the liner's morse lamp high on the truck of her lofty main-mast, left an undying impression in my youthful mind of this quiet, eventful and beautiful hour. The hissing grumble of her bow wave and the swishing splatter of her engine exhaust water as she swept past, with the sight of hundreds of passengers at her rails, only served to emphasize her luxurious activity and our sparse loneliness.

Years later I saw a coloured shipping company's poster depicting a large passenger liner ablaze with electric lights, passing on a moonlit sea a solitary, darkened, sailing ship whose sails reflected dully the brilliance of moonlight and whose port sidelight glowed redly. I remembered then this incident and wondered if the artist had been aboard the liner. The ship was not *Lancing* and the steamer was not the same liner, but maybe the artist had no great choice of museum models.

The Second Mate placed the lamp on the deck close to a ventilator and crossing to the wheel-house trunk where I was standing watching the fast-moving liner crossing our wake, he called softly down the opened flap to the helmsman below and I caught the words, '*Baltic*–White Star–Liverpool'.

* * *

About the beginning of August the ship was approaching the Grand Banks off Newfoundland and I saw the one and only iceberg that I have ever seen over a period of about 13 years of active seafaring. Another 'berg had been passed during the night, after the change of watches, so I had missed it for I was asleep.

The weather had become colder with occasional patches of fog or mist, which brought the hand fog-horn out of the locker and up on the fo'c'sle-head where a pin was removed from the fife-rail abaft the knight-heads and the heavy, oblong box containing the mechanism was mounted there, secured by a turn of the fore topmast staysail downhaul. The groans and howls of this instrument cannot be compared to any known noises. The intensity of pitch depended on the speed with which the handle on the side was rotated. Larvik and I attempted to produce a tuneful melody from the three blasts which were called for but the Captain sent the Second Mate forward to enquire, 'What the hell you think you're doing?'

One afternoon, as we were performing some routine job of work on deck, the big bell sounded three regular clangs and one of two men who happened to be working on the fo'c'sle-head sung out, 'Ice ahead-d-d!' The 'berg must have been concealed by haze which thinned as the ship sailed towards it for it was not long before we came up with it.

It was an inspiring and lonely sight. A 'pinnacle' 'berg rising like a white and ghostly steeple against the haze of the early morning sunlight. A cold, lovely horror floating serenely in the calm waters, towering to a height of about 300 feet from the sea's surface, a glistening menace but a beautiful and strange new sight to me.

The base at the waterline measured roughly a couple of hundred feet square. *Lancing* was running free with the wind right aft and had altered course to starboard when the iceberg had been sighted. She sailed slowly past it at a distance of about three-quarters of a mile because the wind was light and the sea's surface calm with a slight swell. We looked our fill since there was no call yet on our services. Four bells would come soon enough.

The pale daylight glinted and reflected from the towering surfaces of ice, casting shadows in the deep crevasses. Some of the colours within the ice showed varying intensities of green, black and purple. The black had the appearance of rock, trapped within the frigid tomb. The ice was visibly melting as rivulets of liquid like miniature waterfalls cascading from crag to crag revealed white icicles of varied thicknesses and lengths depended from the small overhanging cliffs.

The sea on the weather side foamed and broke in disarray, washing upwards and falling back on itself leaving momentary, quickly diminishing pools to wash down over the shelving beach of ice, to be met half way by another wave. The sea on the lee side boiled and swirled over submerged reefs and outcrops and, as the back of the 'berg came slowly into view, we saw a cave or cavern low down in which the sea rose and fell, washing in and out with deep sighings. There was no visible appearance of life, not even a seal or a bird, and as it slowly and majestically drifted away astern our eyes followed it from time to time and we wondered if any ship would strike against it in the coming nights.

For the next 12 hours, the subject of ice and its hazards occupied our conversations and I listened to many personal experiences being related, some of which I found hard to credit at that time, 'Whole islands of ice, some as big as the Isle of Man!' But one tale that I knew to be true was that told to the whole fo'c'sle by Pelle, who, while narrating it, laughed at the panic they all got into when *Lancing*, travelling at a fair speed, had collided with an iceberg!

They all thought, once the vessel was stationary and grinding against the side of the 'berg, that she would sink so they hurriedly abandoned her and left in two of the lifeboats, pulling clear to witness her end. Instead of which the ship made a clear turn about and drifted off and the wind filling her sails from aft sent her sailing slowly and grandly away from the 'berg—and the lifeboats!

Pelle said, and was backed up by the other seamen who were in the ship at that time, 'We have one hell of a yob to catch her!' The only damage the vessel sustained was a dented plate below the waterline, which caused a 'weep' in one of the ballast tanks, and a cracked yard truss. I think she was sailing at a speed of about four or five knots and remained alongside the 'berg for 30 minutes, grinding and pounding against the ice, and yet sailed herself off, practically unscathed. As a Lloyds surveyor said of her, 'She is truly one of the Shipping Wonders of the World!'

I listened to this first-hand account with feelings of envy, though I had heard all the details in the Consulate at the time. Why had it to happen before I had joined her? Though everyone connected with the ship knew about the abandonment, I have reason to believe that it was not reported, though the collision was, and it was repeated many times by local reporters in the ports where the ship docked.

Pelle, Larvik and Stavanger related with gusto the incidents during the abandonment and after. How, thinking that the masts would come down and the sails might smother them and hold them to the deck as she sank, they got the lifeboats off the chocks and over the side in record time. When they had pulled away and lay-to to watch her end they discovered that they had no provisions in the boats and worse still—no tobacco! By the time that they had doubled up the crew in one boat and chased the ship, returning aboard with much difficulty because the boat falls had been cut and had unrove, they were all exhausted, soaked in sweat and blisteringly thankful!

*　　　*　　　*

One of my failings was that I sometimes went to sleep while on the lookout. During this voyage I think that I did this about four or five times. Twice I curled up and slept, deliberately! Until *shame* and a bucketful of ice cold water cured me.

The first time it happened I had done about one hour of my watch of two hours' lookout on the fo'c'sle-head and the weather was cold and wet. I was completely exposed to the cutting wind and driving spray while the ship sailed close-hauled to the north-westward. I was damp, cold and miserable and could find no shelter anywhere. The continuous bursts of spray across the open deck was annoying me and I was as tired as any dog. The ship's movement was lively and I was unable to walk more than a few steps before I had to hang on to the rail or the head-sheets to steady myself.

Then I noticed a place right up in the bows which would afford me a little shelter, but it meant lying down on the deck. The ship was fitted with two decorative king-posts, or knight-heads, and the timber supporting these as a brace not only filled the space athwartships above the heel of the bow-sprit but they extended fore and aft on both sides, diminishing in height as they sloped aft and terminated where the scuppers began. I thought that if I lay down on the deck on the weather side I would be sheltered from the worst of the weather and could raise my head occasionally and take a casual look at the horizon.

I did lie down in the only shelter available to me and I found that I was indeed protected from the wind, but not from the spray. Stretched out along the deck I could not see directly ahead but I could pop my head up from time to time and view the expanse of shimmering wet gloom up to windward. I was now relaxed, my muscles were at rest and though still cold and wet I found that I was comfortable at last. Pillowing my cheek on the wet oilskin of my arm, immediately my eyelids drooped. After some weak attempts at keeping them open I permitted them to remain closed and sighed comfortably. This was luxury!

I came to my senses sliding and rolling across the deck and when I tried to struggle upright I could not, because one leg was up in the air somewhere and someone was hanging on to my foot. I was being dragged around the deck by one leg. When I had been used as a mop for some moments my leg was released and I found the Farmer looking down at me. He lifted me to my feet and cuffed me once across the head but it was not a vicious blow.

'You don't go asleep on the look-out, boy,' he exclaimed, not unkindly. I looked him in the face and lied.

'I wasn't asleep—I was resting my eyes—I was only sheltering.' He hit me again and this time it was a real swipe. It hurt.

'Bad enough that you sleep on the look-out but *don't tell lies*!' He ordered me off the fo'c'sle-head for he was my relief.

Another time I deliberately went to sleep in the dark and awoke in daylight. It was the last time too. It was my lookout from 0400 to 0600, and the weather was mild and sultry. We had lost sleep in the previous watch when all hands had been called on deck to tack or wear ship, or perform some manœuvre or other. I knew that my next watch below would be interrupted by breakfast which would consume about half or three-quarters of an hour, and again for dinner which would steal another 30 minutes from our precious four hours off. Before I could turn in after breakfast I would have to clear and wipe down the table, collect the kits, dump the leftovers and return the utensils to the galley. After a very brief watch below I faced the prospect of a long afternoon watch on deck, lasting about six hours!

I determined to get some sleep while I could, so taking a long look round the horizon and a glance at the sidelights, I climbed into the main-topmast staysail netting and blissfully drifted off to sleep.

The netting was spread and secured between the fork of the double mainstay and the afterpart of the foremast. It was like a hammock and was constructed of tarred rope, or 'ratline stuff'. Voices awakened me and I glanced round at the grey daylight in some surprise. As I prepared to climb out of the netting in full view of whoever might be about, I saw loud-mouthed Ed scrambling up the starboard ladder nearby and he was carrying a bucket. Just as I was about to sit up he saw my movement and scurrying towards me gave an obscene shout of triumph and with a hurried swing emptied the contents of the bucket all over me.

I was drenched by cold salt water and was fully awake but I was not afraid of that big 'bag-o'-wind' and I cursed him luridly in English and Norwegian while keeping myself poised for instant retreat should he offer violence. Some of the other seamen of my watch had followed him to see the fun and the crowd of them laughed loudly at the spectacle of my discomfort. I was furious! Not because I had been caught and punished but simply because the person who had administered it was a man whom I despised. A man who claimed to be a sailorman but who was himself disgraced. Had he not been sent from the wheel because he could not steer?

I felt more hurt and mortified over that circumstance than I did of sleeping on the look-out. The punishment was a bitter one at his hands and it rankled long after. But it was the last time that I dared to close my eyes while on watch. There was no way of knowing *who* would awaken me or *how*!

The young Finn in the port watch lost quite a bit of sleep in his efforts to catch me asleep on the lookout. His head would slowly rise up at the break of the fo'c'sle-head and as slowly be withdrawn. I saw this happen several times, especially when I was leaning against something and not walking about. I derived considerable satisfaction at the thought of all the precious sleep that I was causing him to lose.

One other thing which did not endear me to that big oaf Ed, was the matter of my bunk curtain. In a fo'c'sle full of humanity there are times when a man wishes to withdraw, to be alone with his thoughts, or just smoke his pipe, gaze on his bare toes and think of whatever is closest to his desires. All seamen like to have some sort of screen to draw across the length of the bunk, or even a short one which encloses about two feet of space at the pillow end so that a shadow is cast across their eyes when they wish to sleep. Some simply drape a towel across the wire and let it go at that.

Curtains are made out of any material which comes to hand. Even a pair of overall pants and a sweat-stained shirt can constitute a screen of sorts. Early in the voyage I decided to make myself a bunk curtain, but I planned to have a sailor-like one, in keeping with my surroundings.

I obtained a length of well-worn soft staysail canvas from the Sailmaker. It was about eight feet in length and, being sailcloth, it was two feet in width. Under Pelle's direction I cut this to the length of my bunk and he gave me a palm, sail-needle and waxed twine and showed me how to sew a two-inch tabling round the edges. I made a small sail of the curtain by stitching loops, or grommets, on the outside and other loops at the lower corners as clews which looped over small bent nails on the bunkboard and prevented the curtain from swinging away from the bunk as the ship heeled to leeward or rolled.

Passing a wire through the head tabling I set it up with a lanyard. My shipmates were now very interested and showed me how to do this. Then I rove off two clewlines and a couple of buntlines, joined them together inside the bunk and led them through a bent nail in the deckhead so that with one pull I could furl my curtain. The able seamen insisted that I complete the job by making a couple of gaskets, so to please them I did so.

I was a proud boy when I demonstrated my completed design. Of course there were many hilarious remarks passed about it and it was quite common to hear, 'Clew yer foresail up, Yack, scoffs on the table,' or, '*Lancing*'s settin' a skysail now—in Yack's bunk. That'll add a couple of knots to her speed!' While somebody would add, 'Aye, on pea-soup-days!'

One afternoon as I was preparing to turn in, big, loud-mouthed Ed entered the fo'c'sle to get something or other from his bunk. I swung my legs into the security of my own bunk, let go the running gear of the curtain and sheeted home the clews.

I heard Ed passing obscene observations about the curtain in hilarious tones. Suddenly the canvas bulged inwards to a violent blow, the blade of a sheath knife appeared before my eyes and slid downwards cutting a foot long gash in the curtain's centre! I looked through the gap and saw Ed, the big, ignorant buffoon, scrambling hastily across the table back to his side of the fo'c'sle, knife in hand. He turned with screeching laughter and contorted features, shouting, 'All hands on deck, foresails carried away!'

I seemed to feel the hair on my head stand up stiffly. But it was only my boyish mind sending out useless prayers to the gods to give me soon, oh, so soon, the body and the strength of a man, to defend my ideals and my way of life from the encroachment of stupid, greedy and ignorant individuals!

As he giggled his way out of the fo'c'sle, past seamen in their underwear who asked him *why* he had done it, I cursed him in the choicest words of an augmented vocabulary, words that I had long been afraid to utter aloud, lest I bring down the wrath of heaven upon myself, and some other words which I was only now aware that I knew.

I did not attempt to repair the gash. Perhaps I figured that if I did so, Ed would only repeat the offence. If I left it as it was maybe he would be satisfied. Perhaps I was right for he did not bother me again.

Ed was an obnoxious type of shipmate, like the young Finn and the poor half-witted creature in the dark lower bunk, though the Finn was a real good sailorman and well worth his rating in the ship. Ed had had training of a sort and may well have matured with age. He may later have had experiences which shocked him into taking a serious view of his way of life. Perhaps he developed into a good and efficient seaman, perhaps master of some steamer, who knows? Such things do happen and I hope that he made a success of his life—or died bravely.

Lancing was manned and sailed by professional seamen for the most part, and for this I am thankful. I am glad that the ship went to her end when she did (1925) for had she sailed the seas for a further decade we would have had a whole generation of ex-lieutenants, publicans, university students and graduates, photographers and journalists, male and female politicians, fashion models and the bearded, pipe-wearing, shilling-a-month passage workers, all boring us with their reminiscences of, 'a grand, tough life in the old square-riggers, old man!' or 'around the Horn with me!'

4. *Lancing* in the First World War.

5. *Lancing* sailing on the starboard tack, wind over the quarter and travelling at speed. What appears to be a royal yard lashed in the lee scuppers suggests the period to be sometime after 1921 (copyright Mrs P. Pedersen).

6. *Pereire* (later re-named *Lancing*) as she was built in 1865—a single-funnel barque-rigged screw steamer, owned by the Compagnie Générale Transatlantique.

7. *Pereire*, in her second form, with two funnels and increased horsepower (both from Collection Transatlantique).

CHAPTER TEN

Canada in Sight

One rain-wet, misty morning I was working aloft with the big
Russian. We were sitting astride the starboard fore upper
t'gallant yard-arm. I do not remember the nature of the job but
I think it must have involved the royal sheet. The ship was running free with a moderate wind over the starboard quarter and
sometimes the sun broke through the low and heavy clouds
bringing occasional dry spells and showing brilliantly coloured
soft rainbows arching down to the sea.

My eyes were as usual straying from the job in hand and
drinking in the sights of the morning, the uneven patches of
horizon through mist, the decks and people far below, the sails
on the other masts and the tracery of rigging against the sea.
Looking ahead and to leeward I saw a two-masted schooner.
Excitedly, I pointed it out to the Russian who gazed casually
and said, 'A Bluenose fisherman, and there's another under his
lee.' I had concentrated too much on the first vessel so had
missed seeing the other. He then told me about the Grand
Banks fishing fleets of fast sailing schooners out of Halifax,
Lunenberg, Boston and other Canadian and American ports,
finishing up with the surprising information that the two
schooners might be rum-running!

This put me in a fever of excitement and tremendous interest
so that I could not take my eyes off the pair of graceful schooners
beating up towards the north. They had low, black hulls and
dazzling white canvas and reminded me of the pictures I had
seen of slavers sailing the 'Middle Passage'. I was sure in my
own mind now that they were rum-runners and I was prepared
to inform all my ex-school friends, when I returned home,
that I had seen rum-runners! My eyes strained towards the
schooners, looking astern of them for the chasing gunboat

H   113

which should be firing on them now, but there was no such craft tearing across the seas in short bumps, throwing wide, high sprays aside. Pity.

Several years later, I did sail in a rum-runner, a big, wooden, five-masted Canadian schooner fitted with auxiliary engines and it was two of the happiest and most interesting years that I spent under sail in the Pacific Ocean.

The two graceful schooners gradually fell astern of us and disappeared into the mist while the Russian told me all that he knew about Rum Row, three miles off the coast of New Jersey, U.S.A. It was not much but it was full of interest.

Three years later I was to see it for myself, from the decks of a steamer in which I was serving as an officer cadet. It was a busy, bustling, rowdy sight, like a street market dumped down in the sea with vessels of all types and rigs, from large steam yachts to four-masted schooners, anchored in plain sight of the towers of Manhattan and with giant blackboards hanging overside giving a visual description of their wares with the current prices, while fast motor launches lay off, or alongside, bargained, loaded and ran for it in full view of the slow, and at that time decrepit, cutters of the U.S. Federal Law Enforcement Agency whose duty it was to shoot it out and capture the heavily armed and well-manned high-speed launches of the rum-runners. As may be imagined there were few successful actions in the early days.

The job completed we were about to return to the deck when, looking over the left shoulder of my Russian shipmate and friend as he passed the lanyard of his tool bag over his head, I saw a big three-masted full-rigged ship sailing out of the mist to starboard, following the same course as us. I made haste to tell him about the strange vessel.

Twisting around on the yard-arm he scrutinized the stranger.

'She is one of ours, Russian,' he said. 'She is *Grand Duchess Maria Nikolaevna* and before that she was the British ship, *Hesperus*, a clipper and a fast sailer. We all call her just *Duchess*. She is school ship for Navy. I think when she is British, she carry passengers. See the long poop deck?' He hailed the deck and gave the information, 'Sail-l-l O-o-oh!' but our people must have seen her because several climbed into the starboard rigging, gazing out on the beam.

The *Duchess* was an iron ship with the same lack of sheer as *Lancing*. Her tonnage would be about 2,000 deadweight. She was painted grey, the colour most favoured by penny-pinching shipowners, but once she had been port-painted over a black hull, like *Lancing*, with white lower masts and doublings and white bands on black yards. Now she looked like a grey ghost. Truly, I was looking at the spectre of a vanishing era, had I but known it.

We watched the ship sail into a sunlit patch of sea and become alive and swept by shadows. Her wet grey-white sails glistened as she leaned over slightly towards us and I noticed then that she was altering course away from us. Her fore-yards were moving round in small jerks as her seamen hauled on the braces and within a very short time all her yards were braced at a steeper angle than ours but she still appeared to keep about the same station with us.

She carried that fine looking, but unhandy, spar, a jib-boom over the bowsprit and set double topsails on the fore, main and mizzen, with double t'gallant sails on the fore and main, but a single on the mizzen. I thought that this latter sail looked odd and slightly out of place when viewed with the sails on the other masts, but the Russian told me that it was common practice in many ships of her tonnage and rig. She carried several boats below lofty davits which were fitted to the shell plating on the outside of the hull. She had all plain sail set except the cro'jack. Like us, she carried royals, and as we watched, we saw her upper staysails rise swiftly up the stays and be sheeted home.

She sailed almost neck and neck with us for about an hour, gradually drawing further and further away and I liked to think that I was taking an active part in a race between these two old ships. Finally we saw her merge into a bank of mist or rain and disappear. We never saw her again.

* * *

The Sunday previous to our arrival at Cape Chat, our destination, the Donkeyman entered the fo'c'sle during breakfast and informed me that I was to assist him in cleaning out the steam donkey boiler. 'It will take all day an' as you're the smallest boy in the ship, the Second Mate says you're to go inside it an' chip off the scale. Put yer old clothes on!' I was under the impression that all my clothes were old, so this last remark had the effect of giving me a better opinion of my wardrobe. 'The Donkey' departed and then the agitators got to work on me.

It was pointed out, of course, that it was my watch on deck from 0800 to noon but this was a Sunday.

'You should get overtime for dat job, Yack,' said one.

'Ya, ya, Sunday vork, iss all overdime in sheeps now. Dat iss sea law!' declaimed another, while someone else waved a thick finger and offered me advice.

'You tell Second Mate, Yack, dat if you don' get overtime you don' do da yob!' I shivered at the thought. Another voice was raised and found general agreement.

'Anyhow, the job ain't sailorizing, it's up to Donkey to do it 'imself, 'e gits paid for it!'

I felt heartened at all this. I did not want the rotten job, though I did not object to the nature of the work itself. It was the idea of *me* working on a Sunday while the rest of my shipmates had the day off! The money for working overtime did not interest me at all. It was leisure I wanted, not work. The small amount of money that I might gain in addition to my meagre wages would not come to me until I paid off; a long time to wait. However, I seemed to have general support and these men who spoke to me were, after all, my shipmates, so I finished my breakfast and sat on my seachest smoking a cigarette—and waiting.

Two bells were struck aft and answered by the big bell forward whose clanging penetrated through all the fabric of the deck-house wherein I sat. It sounded to me like the bell in Duke Street Prison that tolled under the black flag on the moment of execution. The Donkeyman appeared at the doorway nearest me.

'All right, Peasoup, you come topside now.' He always used this one of my three nicknames. I said to him, 'Do I get overtime for this job?' He appeared shocked, and stared in wonder at me. When I did not rise, he turned on his heel and went away. Again I waited while the rest of the seamen became engaged in various trivial occupations. Two or three went out on deck.

The Second Mate appeared and stepped into the fo'c'sle.

Looking at me he crooked a finger. 'Boy, go with the Donkey-man!' I swallowed hard and stood up. In a rather high-pitched and strange voice I asked, 'Do I get overtime on this job, sir?' I only wanted him to say loudly, so the others would hear, 'no-you-don't,' and put an end to my misery, but he did not. His blue-grey eyes bored into mine and his mouth tightened as he reached out an arm like a hawser. His big hand closed firmly on my shoulder.

'Overtime?' he asked in amazement and I ducked because I thought that he was about to take a swipe at me. His eyes left my face and his gaze travelled slowly round the entire fo'c'sle, then he looked back at me and pushed me towards the port doorway. Letting go of my shoulder he gestured with his other hand, thumb outstretched. 'On deck, boy!' No one had spoken but me and the officer.

The realization came at last: that deck boys in sailing ships have absolutely no rights whatever, and I joined the Donkey-man on top of the deck-house. Before instructing me in my duties he questioned me about the events in the fo'c'sle during breakfast. I told him and he laughed when I gave the names of the men who had encouraged me to ask for overtime. 'Oh, them!' His tone showed his distaste. As three hearty blasts of the officer's whistle cut through the quiet Sunday sunshine, the Donkeyman spoke. 'Now you see something!' As my watch assembled at the lee jigger braces, he said, 'You're all right, you stay here with me.' He grinned cheerfully.

The sheet-iron cover of the top of the boiler casing had been removed and the elliptical steel manhole door of the boiler crown was off. This lay aside, secured loosely by a rope-yarn to one of the stud bolts so that it would not slide and fall down into the donkeyroom below. I looked inside the boiler and received a shock. I had thought boilers were just tanks which were full of water, which, when heated by the fire in the bottom, turned the water into steam which powered the winches. This one appeared to be full of steel tubes from top to bottom, close-packed and vertical. There were four narrow segmented spaces between the square grid of tubes and the radius of the boiler shell and it was into these that I had to go. With a blunt chipping hammer I had to chip off all the loose rust from the inside of the shell and collect it from the bottom of the boiler, scraping it together into an old shirt (one of mine) and passing it up to the Donkeyman for disposal. I was reminded of the boys in the tales of Charles Dickens who performed similar work for chimney-sweeps.

As I climbed down into the boiler, shoeless as instructed, I saw the watch on deck hauling away at the lee main braces, trying to gain an inch on a brace already bar taut! When they had belayed the fore braces, the Second Mate would shout, 'That'll do the watch!' and the seamen would relax and go back to their Sunday occupations, washing clothes, mending or making shoes, patching shirts or overalls, or just sitting on the hatches in small groups, talking.

The officer would give them ten minutes or less, then the whistle would shrill out again and they would try to gain an inch on the sheets. After another false rest period the whistle would again disturb the serenity prevailing. This time it would be the tacks of the courses, or the halliards! And so the morning passed with the watch on deck moving from one unnecessary job to another. It was called 'hazing' and is a form of punishment against which there is no legal redress, for the officers' opinion of the state of the sails and gear is unquestionable.

The Donkeyman looked down on my labours, the shadow of his head darkening the inside of the boiler. 'Peasoup, your watch getting plenty overtime now—an' not gettin' paid for it either!' He laughed and chuckled.

The inside of the boiler stank of wet rust and stagnant water, like the ballast tanks. I had a minimum of space in which to move and I could only stand upright. My feet had no real grip since the bottom of the boiler was curved downwards, or dished. My feet found the horizontal braces which were bolted round the tubes but they were too narrow, and painful to stand on. My back was against the tube grid and my chest within a couple of inches of the curved shell. When one hand became tired with using the hammer to tap off the blue-russet scale, the only way that I could change the hammer to the other hand was to contract the muscles of my stomach and pass the hammer through the gap. When I slid down to the lower end of the boiler to collect the rust scale in the shirt, I had to contort my legs and feet, to get them under the grid for I could not bend down far enough, or turn around.

It was a hell of a job. My shirt under my arms impeded the few possible movements so I stretched both arms upwards and the Donkeyman pulled the garment off me. I was covered with slimy rust stains, my knuckles were sore and bleeding and my stomach and chest bore bruises from the end of the hammer shaft. When I tapped the shell a few microscopic bits of adamantine slag *might* be detached. The Donkeyman tried to cheer me up, since he guessed from the hollow curses reaching his ears, that I was a bit apathetic about the whole thing. 'You'll get extra allowance of fresh water for a bath, when we finish the job!' I disliked the sound of that *we*, he in the sunshine and me in the hole. All *he* was doing was lounging across the blasted crown of the boiler and talking.

Maybe he took pity on me, for about six bells he stuck his head inside, said that it looked fairly clean and really did not require scaling and I could leave the other side wall alone and come out. I wormed my painful way up the tubes, he grabbed my wrists and hauled me out into the clean, fresh, cool day, where I rested my filthy, bruised and sweating body and panted with sheer relief!

I noticed that my watch were again busy on deck. We put the man-hole cover on top of the gasket and I succeeded in getting one of my fingers jammed under the cover. My yell brought instant release. Later the nail turned black and I lost it. It was now my turn to watch the Donkeyman work. While he screwed the nuts on to the stud bolts and hardened them down with a big spanner, I idled my time away watching my shipmates work hard and sullenly down on the main deck.

The casing cover was replaced and *we* had finished the job by one bell in spite of a forecast of a day's work ahead for us. The stack, or funnel, was already in place at the side of the boiler flue, having been previously bolted on by the port watch.

I think that it was about this time that the dog disappeared. One night it was aboard the ship, in the morning it was not! No search was instituted since it was fairly obvious what had occurred. No questions were asked of the foremast hands, as I think now, that the afterguard had found from experience that dogs, like billiard tables, have no place in a ship at sea.

As *Lancing* neared the Canadian coast, we had been touching up the paint-work about the deck-houses and bulwarks. The old Chief Mate had had the lee side of the poop deck painted. It was a yellow ochre colour and looked fresh and bright, like new wood. This happened to be the port side, and the deck was canvas-covered. The line of demarcation between the old dry canvas and the fresh wet paint followed exactly the centreline of the ship.

The paint had been applied in the morning watch, between 0800 and noon, with the Chief Mate carefully supervising the able seamen who performed the work. The watches changed at midday and the warm afternoon wore away quietly. Shortly before 1600, I mounted the after ladder to the poop and was met by a scene of consternation!

The old Chief Mate was pacing up and down the deck, his face turned to the skies while wailing curses poured from his lips as he held his clenched and shaking fists in front of him. I looked for the cause of all this and there on the freshly painted deck, all over it in wavering, searching trails were the prints of a dog's pads! The Second Mate stood aside, silent, withdrawn and helpless, red of face beneath the tan while wrath ebbed and flowed as he stamped his feet in our vicinity. From the sounds I suspected that he was using Swedish, in addition to the Norwegian and Danish curses hovering around us and which he was choosing to give expression to his emotion. I had to admire the man! The damage had all been done while the Second Mate was writing up the log-book in the saloon. Next day—the dog had gone.

As the ship neared the end of her transatlantic passage some of the ballast tanks were pumped out. In this new, dry summer weather with quiet seas and bright sunshine, we worked on them. When a tank had been pumped out, the lid was removed and of course there was still a good quantity of water which had lain beyond the reach of the strum-box, owing to the heel of the vessel while sailing, so an ordinary seaman and a boy went into the bilges to collect it and dry out the tank.

A wire span was rigged between the masts, a steel cargo block shackled to it and a wire whip rove off through the block. A rope guy was added which was led to a pin on the mainrail then the rig was hove aloft until, when everything was set up taut, the whip plumbed the ballast tank. A heavy manila rope strop was fitted and lashed to a big wooden cask and shackled to the whip. Steam had been raised in the donkey boiler to pump out the tanks, so the whip was brought to the winch drum and the cask lowered into the tank, filled by buckets, and hove up on deck again by means of the steam winch.

The cask was brought to the hatch coamings and the Second Mate, Stavanger, and I tipped it up and allowed the stinking contents to spill over the iron main deck. Larvik was driving the winch but when my size and strength proved inadequate for tipping the heavy cask across the coamings, they showed me how to drive a steam winch, a simple task, and Larvik was pressed into the deck work.

I felt intensely proud and very useful and, after a couple of mistakes which were due to a too-rapid reaction to a shouted order and a too slow one to a signal given by the officer's nodding head instead of his hand, I managed all right, once I had overcome my fear of disgrace if I should be so unfortunate as to do something *stupid*.

One forenoon I turned out of my bunk at seven bells (1130), rather early for me, but it happened to be pea soup day, one of the two days in the week when I gorged myself on this alone and subsequently floated stiffly about the decks and clawed my painful and laborious way aloft on a bowel-full of wind. Armed with a discarded enamel bowl which I had been given by some kind-hearted shipmate as being a better utensil for soup than a plate, I was ladling out pints of it with my mug when someone called through an open port, 'Seen the land yet? It's under the lee.'

Banging the bowl down on the table and dropping my mug into it I shot out of the fo'c'sle. Being far too small to see over the high bulwarks I ran swiftly up the starboard ladder to the fo'c'sle-head and looked to leeward. At first I could see nothing and asked the others, 'Where the hell's the land?' It was pointed out to me. A low smudge of dark hazy material far out on the starboard beam. '*That's* Canada?' I was disappointed. I had expected to see the Heights of Abraham or something similar, about a hundred yards ahead of the bowsprit with elevated trains, trolley cars, taxis and people, all dashing about their business round the bases of large concrete buildings.

During the night the look-outs were doubled and we were warned to look for masses of floating logs. The lights of moving shipping kept the big bell striking intermittently. When day-light dawned we were still in sight of land to starboard but it was much nearer now. Rolling green hills covered with trees and scrub with a surf breaking against rocks on the foreshore but no signs of any habitation. No houses, no log cabins, no Indian canoes, no forest fires, not even a smoke signal.

Gradually the land fell away and disappeared. The next time that I saw land we were called out to shorten sail and stand by to anchor while whole masses of land were stretched out along the port beam as far as the eyes could reach. We were sailing slowly into the green coast where there were frame houses and other types of larger buildings, also of wood, with columns of smoke trails rising and spreading from brick chimneys and steel stacks.

I was aloft with most of the crew when we heard the cable running out as we furled the sails. The rattling song of the cable promised a night in for all of us, except the watchman. Finished with watch-and-watch for a week or two now!

The smell of the land was stronger now, and attractive, after the long days of the working scents of a sailing ship which surrounded our living.

The noise of the cable had ceased and now the big full-rigged ship slowly swung round head to wind and stretched her cable over the bottom as she made sternway with all sails aback. Another rattling length of chain danced over the windlass gypsy and was brought up all standing as Chips screwed the brake bands tight and finished the job with a few taps of his maul.

We aloft now had the difficult job of furling sails which were all aback. The wind, now dead ahead, pressed the heavy sails against our toecaps as we stood on the foot-ropes and the canvas was flattened against the forepart of the yards as we tried to coax a crease in sails which were like boards and out of sight below us. But gradually we managed to get the sails on the yards, putting a harbour stow on each, then we trailed around the decks squaring the yards and aligning them with the lifts in a seamanlike manner.

As the shore lights in the houses winked into being we ate our supper to the damp smell of vegetation, wood smoke and the scent of pines, while the eerie silence on an anchorage was all about the resting ship. Pelle and the new nightwatchman, Larvik, hoisted the heavy anchor-light on the fore topmast staysail halliards and its wan and flickering illumination danced across the still decks and the bare, shorn spars. We had reached Canada!

CHAPTER ELEVEN

Loading the cargo of Spoolwood

The ship had come to an anchor off Cape Chat after a fairly uneventful passage of 30 days from Ardrossan. She lay about two miles offshore on an exposed part of the coast of the Gaspé Peninsula in the Gulf of St Lawrence.

We boys, with the able assistance of Big Ed and under the supervision of the Chief Mate, Mr Larsen, man-handled the accommodation gangway off the boatskids where it was stowed, swung it over the starboard side abaft the mizzen back-stays, rigged it and lowered it into position. We had first removed a section of the t'gallant rail and on either side of the gap we set up and bolted two carved brass-crowned teak-wood posts which gave a decorative entrance to the ship, then we finished by lashing the inboard ladder in place, this also having its quota of brasswork.

While we were busy, the Second Mate, the Carpenter and the Sailmaker were erecting 'dollies' or wooden bits along the port rail. I sometimes heard them referred to as 'noks' and they were simply pieces of tree trunks with the bark still on them and they measured about four feet in length by nine inches in diameter. They were horizontal belaying-pins and were fixed tight up under the mainrail by dogged timbers, wedges and fore-and-aft wire lashings, they were then immovable and were inspected every morning by the Carpenter and the Mates. They resembled wooden gun barrels pointing inboard.

The bo'suns and able seamen rigged the cargo gear, which consisted of a loose wire span between the masts with a steel gin block plumbing the hatchway, through which was rove a manila rope fall called the 'midship'. A wire fall led from the winch, up through a gin block and out to another at the cock-billed yard-arm, then back down on deck where a cargo hook was shackled to it. This wire was called the 'yard-arm'. The midship fall was now shackled to the single cargo hook while its free end was led to the dollie. This timber dollie was polished and smooth as silk before the first day of loading had passed.

The method of loading cargo with only one power winch at each hatch was simple. The yard-arm fall raised the load from the lighter alongside, as high as was deemed necessary while at the same time the seaman on the midship fall took in all the slack he could then caught about four turns of rope round the dollie and held on. Then, as the winch went into reverse and slacked away, the weight of the load came on the midship fall and the sling-load of cargo travelled inboard until it was over the hatchway, both falls lowered together, and the cargo descended into the hold. When discharging cargo the rig was still the same but the midship was led to the winch and the yard-arm to the dollie.

It was a fairly rapid method of working cargo but it called for accuracy when landing the load, since once landed it could not be lifted and moved to another position. However, due to the smallness of the average sailing ship hatches it did not matter much. The hatches were not the only means whereby cargo entered the holds of a sailing ship for most of them were fitted with bow or stern ports. These were large, watertight ports or square hinged doors in the shell plating and if situated forward they would be under the catheads on each bow, if aft, they would be part of the buttock plating. The fitting of these was to facilitate the loading of long objects with which the hatches were unable to cope, such as long logs, steel rails or similar objects. The ports were hinged at the top, opened outwards and, when closed, were bolted throughout in similar manner to a deeptank lid, except that flush-headed bolts in countersunk holes were used.

When the ship had anchored the previous day, we had been welcomed by the arrival alongside of two motor boats carrying various personages who boarded us and stayed for some considerable time before re-embarking and returning ashore. One of the men was probably a doctor but he did not examine us, another was maybe an immigration clerk who wanted to examine the Carpenter, as he was leaving us there, for he was called aft later on, while another was probably the agent for

J. & P. Coates who supplied the cargo of spoolwood which we were to load and take back to Ardrossan. I have no idea who the others were but probably they were from the Customs.

One of the motor boats was a typical North American work-boat. The kind that would be used for towing logs one day and fishing the next, or carrying a load of gasoline in drums to some remote fishing village. She was about 50 feet overall by 13 feet beam with a raised foredeck, a big pilot house and broad afterdeck carrying a square transom stern.

The other small vessel was a motor cruiser or yacht and about the same dimensions as the work-boat. She did not have a wheel-house as I remember, but she had a raised fore-deck and cabin trunks which left practically no deck space to move about on. She was fitted with a cockpit aft. The work-boat was painted grey over all but the yacht had a white hull with varnished trunking. I forget the names of these two vessels but the yacht had her port of registry, Matane, in large blue letters across the transom. We did not see much of the yacht except on the two Sundays and again on sailing day but the work-boat was a frequent visitor. She was the tug which brought the loaded scows to us and towed away the empties.

The hold was ready to receive cargo and early in the day I noticed the tug approaching. She was towing a loaded scow which was made fast to her starboard side and on top of the cargo were two barrels and about a dozen colourful individuals standing around and watching us. They wore highly-coloured plaid mackinaw jackets with belts of the same material while their trousers were tucked into laced and buckled, high loggers' boots while on their heads they wore small, gaily-coloured, woollen stocking caps. When I had the opportunity to make a closer inspection of these people I thought that many of them had a sweaty and unwashed appearance. Their faces were clean enough under the tan but I sensed that below the neck they had not had a bath for some considerable time. Their hair was black and greasy-looking and most of them could have benefited by a haircut. They were, for the most part, big men over five feet ten inches while those who were not were runty individuals, short and broad like the average seaman.

The scow was a wooden barge, tarred on the bottom, grey-painted and wedge-shaped at both ends. There was not a curved line in her construction but she was ideal for the purpose for which she was built. Wall-sided, flat-bottomed, down-sloping square ends with a small mooring deck above each. She would be about 50 feet overall by 16 beam and ten foot depth of hold. She had no ceiling above the bottom frames.

In response to the signals of the Second Mate who stood on the mainrail, the tug turned head to stream and berthed the scow alongside our port side, forward of the main rigging and abeam of the main hatch. We caught her lines and made her fast. The colourful gang of longshoremen now climbed aboard and I thrilled at their appearance and proximity. These were the types that I had seen in the moving pictures and had read about. They were exactly the same as portrayed in the illustrations of the *Boys Own Paper* and other adventure magazines, except that their feet were not so broad and flat as the artists had made them and they did not wear moccasins or carry Winchester rifles, though I noticed that the toecaps of their boots were shaped and sewn like moccasins.

They brought their barrels aboard and made their headquarters under the fo'c'sle-head. The barrels were upended and stowed between the anchor cables on the forepart of the windlass and when they were opened we found that one contained fresh ships' biscuits and the other molasses. The sweet smell of this syrup was to remain with us until the ship sailed away from Quebec Province.

These men were here to help us load the cargo, so that all three hatches would be working at the same time. I found that amongst themselves they spoke a different language. I was told that it was a French *patois* and though I listened eagerly I could not distinguish a single word, except '*oui*' and '*non*'. The speech was blurred and strange to my uninformed ears; not like the French we had been battered with at school. When they spoke English they talked slowly and exactly, as though each word and sentence were taken down from a shelf, blown upon and presented to the hearer like a gift. Their English had such a strong French accent that, to my young ears, it sounded more French than French.

The French-Canadians camped out under the fo'c'sle-head during our break for the noon meal and returned to the shore each evening at six o'clock. I do not remember them having a midday meal but I think they must have had something in addition to the biscuits and molasses. They worked in the scows and down the mizzen hatch, loading the afterpart of the ship while we loaded and stowed the cargo in the main and mizzen hatches. The longshoremen worked together as a team, mainly I think because of the language. One of them informed me that I spoke very good English and asked where I had picked it up. Without thinking, I replied, 'At school.'

A couple of net slings were tossed down into the scow and the French-Canadians there loaded it. The load was then raised and brought aboard, lowered into the hatch and landed on the tank tops. One able seaman was in each tank while a boy landed the sling, emptied the timber out and fed it to the seaman in the ballast tank.

I was put to this work. Whitey, the coloured seaman, was down in the starboard tank and I was passing the bundles of spoolwood down to him. Each wired bundle of white birch sticks was, to me, heavy and awkward to handle because I was small. The bundles varied in length, but were usually uniform in width and depth. I think the sizes varied between two feet, three feet and five feet long while all were about ten by twelve inches; the individual sticks were about one and a quarter by one and a quarter inches.

Winch drivers and hatchmen were made up of our own able seamen, except in the jigger hatch where the longshoremen worked. In my ignorance I resented this. I thought that it was a waste of a strong man's energy to be sitting at a winch in the sunshine while I, a small boy, was sweating my guts out down in the gloomy, dusty hold. I thought that the system would be improved enormously by putting the able seamen down the hatch and letting *me* drive the winch!

Three scows were now alongside and when work finished for the day, I for one, had had enough. With stooping, lifting, pulling and reaching my back ached and the muscles of my arms and legs felt flayed while my forearms, chest and stomach were chafed red with carrying the bundles. It is surprising how dirty one can become when handling clean timber. The sun was still there when I climbed out of the hatch and staggered to the ship's rail to take a look at Canada, as a welcome change from its industrial product and the painted ironwork of the hold.

A long look at the mirrored surface of the St Lawrence River decided me and stripping off my overalls and singlet I climbed down the ship's side and boarded the scow which was half-empty. Some of the seamen who had witnessed my disrobing act leaned over the rail watching me. The setting sun was warm on my naked body and taking a light breath of the clean air, and, I hoped, to the admiring glances of the audience above, I dived off the scow in a graceful arc.

As I hit the water I felt I had plunged into the Arctic Ocean by mistake. If my head had been above the surface I would have yelled blue murder. The water was ice cold! In my heated state it was a wonder I did not double up with cramp. I shot to the surface and emerged with an explosive gasp and a cry of horror! My shipmates above called down, 'Cold?'

As I looked up at them I found that I was drifting past the ship. I had not noticed that there was a current. By this time two more deck boys, naked as I was, were on the scow so I hastened to swim back to it calling out the black lie, that the water was not bad at all! I found, when I reached the scow and they had plunged into the water, that I had omitted to safeguard my way of retreat by hanging a rope over the side before I had left the safety of its deck, which was now about six feet above the surface of the river.

One of the able seamen slid down and dropped a line over the side of the scow and as I climbed up it I listened to the yells of fright coming from my fellow bathers. Once in the sun I felt warmer and because I was nude the water drained from me very quickly. I was joined by the two other swimmers and we jumped and skipped around the scow and its cargo, in order to restore our circulation or, perhaps, just because we were boys!

The negro, my fellow worker in the ballast tank, now slid down to where we were and plunged into the icy water. I followed him in, not because I wanted to, but I would not have the audience think that I was afraid of the cold water.

Next morning, about ten o'clock, I was feeding the last of a sling-load of spoolwood bundles down to Whitey in the tank when a loaded sling coming aboard landed, by some miscalculation, on the edge of the hatch coaming. Before it could be checked the net had opened out and spilled half of its contents down into the hold. I heard warning shouts and looked up to see the half-empty net hanging over the coamings and an avalanche of spoolwood bundles descending straight down on me. I let go of the bundle I was holding but before I could jump clear the falling timber crashed around me. I felt the shock of blows on various parts of my body as I was pitched across the tank coaming, grasping at empty air. My fingers contacted hard metal and clutched desperately. My senses returned and I found that I was rolling over the coaming. As I dropped inside and the weight came on my arms I could no longer support my weight with one hand as my other shoulder was numb from a blow so I fell into the tank, a distance of about six feet. I think I landed on my back and shoulders on top of the close-packed lumber cargo.

Whitey was bending over me but I had no breath left to answer his questions regarding my welfare. Men's voices were calling down to the negro and when I was able to breathe properly I scrambled to my feet, feeling sore in parts and a bit shaky but otherwise unhurt.

Whitey boosted me out of the tank and we got on with the work. Later, at the fo'c'sle inquest I was informed that I "ad the luck of a pox-doctor!' At least 20 heavy bundles of spool-wood had crashed down on me from a height, yet not one had landed on me directly. They had bounced on the deck, opened out and ricocheted against me and that was all. I felt sore in parts when I turned in that night but I was gratified at the spot-light of publicity which my near squeak brought me. The Cook gave me a small loaf of bread and he and the Sailmaker lounged awhile in the fo'c'sle, talking with the able seamen about the accidents they had seen and entering into such gory details that I could almost smell the antiseptic.

The following morning, feeling stiff but otherwise in good health, I decided to lay up and have a couple of days' holiday on the strength of my accident. When the rest of the crew turned to at four bells I remained in my bunk, conscious that *this time* I had a good excuse! The Bo'sun's Mate had been notified regarding the precarious state of my health and I listened happily to the sounds of activity out on deck. Steam blowing water through the opened drain cocks under the winch cylinders, the tramping of booted feet on the iron deck, the whirr of a block sheave, calls of men and the accelerated thump and knocking of a steam winch starting up.

A shadow darkened the doorway and the Second Mate appeared. He came alongside the bunk and I assumed what I thought was a pain-wracked and pitiful expression on my features. I prepared to explain and describe my condition in answer to his queries and I would finish by weakly being brave about the whole matter and say that I thought maybe I would be able to turn to the day after tomorrow. I looked at his eyes and thought, 'Well no—perhaps tomorrow.' His arm reached into the bunk and a big hard hand grasped my shoulder. I was dragged out forcibly and slapped about three times with an open palm! 'Get into your working gear and turn to down below.' As I sought to regain my breath he said further, 'You're not sick, get to work!'

As I toiled with Whitey in the hold I fumed at the injustice of the governing body. How the hell could he know I was not sick? I might have serious internal injuries, bleeding inwardly, or something? I resolved to investigate this possibility on my next visit to the lavatory. Later in the day, the Second Mate grinned cheerfully and asked about my health. I assured him that I now felt much better.

Slowly the cargo came aboard and crept upwards in the tanks. When it reached the beams under the tanktops we were given large wooden mallets and every space was filled by opening a bundle of suitable length and driving single sticks into every crack and cavity until the cargo occupied every available centimetre of space within the iron hull.

I never saw a rat in *Lancing* and it was no wonder. There was simply no living space for them. Once the ship was loaded to capacity her hull was a solid mass of timber within the shell plating, every tiny space between the beams and frames was filled with timber squeezed tight! I can begin to understand why it was that she did not open her plates when she rammed the iceberg. They had no room to bend inwards.

Loading at this exposed anchorage was interrupted by weather on some occasions, when a squall of wind and rain would blot out the shoreline and send the scows heaving and banging alongside and we would replace fenders and shift the mooring lines on them, so that they would ride clear of our sides in the current. One scow broke adrift and disappeared in a hard rain squall but was found and brought back by the work-boat, half full of water and with some of her cargo afloat inside.

Not being so preoccupied with the need for sleep, we had more leisure in the evenings after work had ceased for the day. We had, of course, the musical sing-songs but some games were played too, suitable to confinement aboard a ship where football was impossible. The majority of these games had a basis of strength-over-skill.

A man would lie flat on his back on the deck and a big wooden capstan bar would be laid lengthwise on his body. He would grip the bar tightly to his chest and loins, keeping his head to one side of it, then attempt to stand upright, without loosening his tight grip on the bar. Since the bar extended down to his feet between his legs and projected beyond his head it required very considerable strength to overcome the leverage exerted by the supine bar on the prone body. It was some years before I could manage this.

Another trick which I found easy to perform was to make a bowline in one end of a single whip, or the hauling part of the royal halliards, then to place your head in the loop of the bowline with the lower part of the rope at the back of the neck, haul yourself off the deck and into the air, where you remained swinging gently like a hanging corpse. It looks gruesome, especially if someone else hauls you up and you can let your arms hang down. But the job must be done with a bowline formed in the rope, otherwise you could really hang yourself. Of course if you look down you fall out of the loop of rope and nearly skin your ears off and it is advisable not to ascend more than ten feet in altitude. You might hurt yourself if you dropped on a hard deck.

Another game frequently played was for two men to sit facing each other on opposite sides of the fo'c'sle table, grasping opposite hands with a firm grip while keeping both elbows in contact with the table, attempt to bend and then force the opponent's arm down flat on the table. This was not the first time that I had seen this bar-room exercise performed, for one of my father's assistants, who had been a Surgeon Lieutenant in the Royal Navy during the war, played it with me often.

A trick that I became rather skilled at was the 'Five Finger Exercise'. This was to press the palm of one hand down flat on the table with fingers outstretched and spread wide and with a sheath knife in the other hand, point downwards, stab down rapidly between each finger, moving the knife from right to left and back again as often as possible. You can pin your finger to the table if you are not strictly accurate, but that is the hazard of the game!

Another sport which appears senseless, but can arouse some admiration in the onlookers, is for two men to sit on seachests facing each other and lash out with booted feet, kicking at each other's shins. This is usually done while wearing leather or rubber seaboots. Surprisingly it is not painful, though every ounce of force is put behind each kick. It is fatigue which determines the loser.

I always had supreme confidence in the ability of the able seamen and when one night after dark, we were grouped around the fo'c'sle table, playing the Five Finger Exercise, the Farmer told me that he could throw a knife the length of the fo'c'sle and place the point accurately between any of my fingers. Believing him, I moved over to the lamp and flattened my left hand palm outwards, against the ends of the midship bunks, waiting for the knife to whizz through the smoky air and bury its point in the wood between my spread fingers.

The Farmer looked at me long and earnestly, then, knife in hand he moved to the fore end of the fo'c'sle. Facing me he appeared to weigh the distance carefully while grasping the knife by the tip of the blade. His arm rose in a slow and graceful arc until the knife was out of my sight behind his head. The seamen sitting round the table rose up hurriedly and moved politely aside, in order to give the knife a clear flight and to safeguard themselves from a ricochet should something go wrong. The Farmer's elbow stopped, steadied and stiffened then his arm shot forward with the speed of light. I jerked my eyes towards my fingers but no knife quivered there.

Looking back at the Farmer I saw that he was grinning somewhat shamefacedly. There was a roar of laughter from all hands and I knew then that I had been the victim of a practical joke. The Farmer had hidden the knife by thrusting the handle of it down inside the neckband of his shirt, behind his head. He now replaced it in the sheath on his belt and resumed his seat while some of the other seamen started to kid me. Again I felt furious at my ignorance and lack of understanding of human nature. When, oh when, would I be able to sort out truth from men's words and actions? I despaired of myself.

In response to the good-natured kidding that poured over me I said, 'But I thought he could throw knives. He *said* he could!' More laughter, and a seaman explained, 'If he could throw knives that good, he wouldn't be aboard here. He'd be in Barnum's Circus, or vaudeville. Gettin' ten or twelve English pounds a week!'

The Farmer, probably noticing my shame, exclaimed. 'Well anyway, he had the guts to stand there an' wait fer it. He didn't pull his hand away at the last minute.' He looked at me, then at them all, and finished, 'As you all thought he would!' I felt immensely cheered by this simple statement. It put me in a better light. Even ignorance can have advantages when allied to that magic respectful word, guts.

CHAPTER TWELVE

Life Aboard whilst Anchored Offshore

By the middle of August the ship was half loaded and one day the Captain entertained guests aboard. There were quite a number of them, about four men, four women, some young girls and three or four children. They all, of course, steered well clear of us forward, keeping to their own end of the ship. The day must have been a Sunday for they were all in their best clothes and I was aloft on the jigger mast taking a look at Canada, instead of being down the hold. As I descended the starboard lower rigging the Captain was watching me as I passed the lifeboat and called out, 'Don't hold on to the ratlines, boy, use the shrouds and you will be safe!'

It is an elementary precaution observed by all seamen that when in the rigging they must use the wire shrouds to hold on to, never the ratlines as the latter have been known to break or carry away, but the shroud never will. Men who use ladders in their work ashore observe the same rule, they grip the sides of the ladder and never the rungs. I had transgressed the rule— and in the presence of the Captain! Being small I had found that as I used the lower rigging both my arms were stretched to an uncomfortable width, since the lower down that the shrouds reached the further they were apart, so I had let go the wire shrouds and clutched the wooden ratline battens. Normally I always observed the usual rule except in the lower rigging where I was handicapped by the short span of my reach.

As I stepped down on to the t'gallant rail Captain Pedersen summoned me to the poop and I thought that I was in for a public reprimand. I made my way to where he stood and instead of admonishing me on my carelessness he introduced me to the ladies as the school friend of Alan Blanner, whom they all remembered.

The females were all seated, some on the skylight, others on the varnished top of the lifebelt box and I thought that they were a colourful lot, who looked and dressed like gypsies. They wore large, flat, gold earrings, dark skirts and brightly coloured blouses and coloured silk head-scarves instead of hats. Only one wore a hat and she was elderly. But I received a pleasant shock when I walked slowly between the seated groups with the Captain who was making the introductions. They had the lowest necklines I had ever seen on women who were not in evening dress. Everything was on view bar the nipples! I bowed low over each introduction and tore my eyes away for the next as I murmured a polite phrase or two. However, the conversation lapsed after the 'Charmed, Madame—Mam'selle—how do you do', as I was very shy with strangers in formal circumstances for I knew that respectable females would have no common ground with me in conversation.

They always talked about things in which I had no interest, such as, '*My*, but you are getting to be quite a *man* now!' or 'I expect you have a young lady now; do you go dancing—and to parties?' As an afterthought, 'Do you like parties? I *love* them!' And, of course, in the presence of the ship's Master, 'And how do you like the ship?'

This formal introduction, apparently on the spur of the moment, was the only privilege that I ever received while I sailed in *Lancing*. Aside from this one isolated incident I was treated for what I was, a deck boy. I expected no favours, sought none and got none. I was perfectly happy to be a professional member of a crew of a big, deep-sea sailing ship. Any ship would have served my purpose, since at my age the fact that *Lancing* was a famous record-holder did not mean a thing to me.

The introductions over, the Captain nodded my dismissal and on my way forward to rejoin my shipmates in the fo'c'sle, glad to have escaped the social round on the poop, I passed the open window of Mr Martin's stateroom where he was entertaining the Captain's male guests, the aroma of whisky was floating forth into the still air, and I heard their laughter.

Though there were no rats or bedbugs in the ship, her fo'c'sle and galley contained whole colonies of cockroaches, or 'steam-flies'. These little insects romped gaily and inquisitively in every bunk, ran up the bulkheads, scuttled across recumbent seamen and explored the heads, chests and beards of sleepers. They marched across the pages of book or magazine and would pause to regard the reader with waving antennae, the females carrying their eggs within a stiff and rigid sack protruding from their backsides like a well-filled seabag.

Noticing the careless familiarity which the other seamen displayed towards these creatures, I, too, grew to ignore them. Where a bedbug would have been instantly squashed to a smelly mass on sight beneath a hard and ruthless thumb, the friendly cockroach was permitted to wander undisturbed and in peace since it never offered hostility to man.

One day while the ship was at sea, the weather being bad at the time, we were eating our dinner under difficulties, balancing and holding on against the steep plunges and swift rolls of the vessel, wedged into odd corners while we consumed the meal. It was a pea soup day and as usual I had no interest in the other edibles. I was shovelling it in, in hasty and large gulps. As the ship rolled steeply to leeward I lifted a spoonful of soup from my bowl which I held under my chin, being a believer in the shortest distance between two points, and, as the liquid drained from the spoon, I noticed a dark object amongst the whole peas but I was too hungry to stop and investigate since it was not uncommon to find a black pea amongst the green. As the soup swam out of the spoon and down my eager throat I recognized too late that it was not a black pea.

Pale and shaken I lowered the bowl and informed my ship-mates in tones of horror and anxious trepidation, 'Hey, I've swallowed a "jasper"!' Some laughed outright while others just grinned. 'Was it carrying eggs?' they asked. When I replied that I thought it was a long one, they said, 'Ya, a female. So the eggs they hatch out in your stomach, and when you are asleep the little babies they come out of your mouth, see?' In my father's books I had read of tapeworms living a lazy life of luxury in the bowels and intestines of human beings, so I was not too sure about what I was hearing now; true maybe?

Someone else embroidered a fancy margin to the tale. 'Ya, ya—that is right. An' the Old Lady she will stay in your stomach for it is warm there an' you keep sending down pea soup to her, so she is all right. But, the little ones will want to go back and visit their mother now an' then, so . . .!' The speaker paused and regarded me. I waited but he did not speak. I finally and suspiciously asked, 'So what?' He finished the sentence, 'So sleep with your bloody mouth shut now!' Someone said cheerfully, 'They can go up his nose and down into his stomach that way.' This was too much for me to credit.

Stavanger remarked, 'You're very lucky.' And when I asked why, said, 'Because you are eating fresh meat while the rest of us have to scoff salt beef an' pork!' Blackbeard came to the rescue. 'Eat your soup, boy, you will come to no harm. If the thing was alive when you swallowed it, it will be dead now. Nothing can live in a boy's stomach except imagination.' Because I wanted to gorge myself on this delicious soup, I was only too happy to believe the words of the fo'c'sle oracle and after a very thorough searching and careful investigation of anything unusual, bringing the bottom layers of soup to the surface with the spoon, I ate the lot in a happy and contented frame of mind.

One Saturday while the ship lay at anchor off Cape Chat, I had occasion to pay a visit to the lavatory during the dinner break. As I entered I looked at the opened port facing me. A thin diagonal line cut across the circular hole in the shell plating. I had seen Pelle streaming a fishing line from the fo'c'sle-head rails in the morning so this must be it. Reaching out my arm and grasping the line I felt it throbbing so hauled away. Suddenly its weight increased and though the port was too small to let my head pass through I did manage to get one eye beyond the rim. About 20 feet below and half out of the water was a big fish.

Standing on the big square wooden seat I hauled away regardless now and with increasing excitement. When the fish reached the lower rim of the port I gingerly passed my arm out beyond his head, because I was afraid that he might bite me, and feeling for the tail which was pressed hard against the shell plating, I succeeded in getting a firm grip on it and with a tremendous heave and a wild shout of triumph and fear, I dragged the scaly monster into the lavatory!

As it came in through the port with a rush I let go everything and the big fish dropped, flapping violently, on to the seat and slid silently down into the pan. Undismayed I hauled it out and holding it carefully by the line I transferred it to the big cask, half-full of seawater which was used for flushing purposes. There it swam around slowly, seeming dazed. I waited until its head was pointing downwards then grabbed its tail and jerked it back on to the seat, but this time I sat over the pan while I shoved the wooden handle of the dipper into its mouth and tried to disengage the hook.

I failed to abstract the hook, so trailing fishing line behind me, I carried the heavy, wet prize into the fo'c'sle and deposited it on the table with pride under the interested gaze of my shipmates. I learned then that it was a cod which weighed about 12 pounds. It was given to the Doctor and appeared next day at supper. I was the only one who did not eat any of it, as I explained when questioned, I was not all that fond of fish and liked mine fried in breadcrumbs or out of a can. Of course, I did not tell them where it went to when I landed it.

Landing this monster of the deep whetted my appetite for more of this sport, so on Sunday afternoon with a borrowed line, I angled from the bottom platform of the accommodation ladder aft. This was an act of daring which I did not fully realize at the time, for the after part of a sailing ship is a sacred precinct given over to the sole use and enjoyment of the Master, Mates and passengers. There is a saying, 'Hogs, dogs and sailor-men got no rights abaft the mainmast.' Normally, all livestock is kept in the forepart of the ship, except chickens, as they lay eggs, for the incumbent aft, who would get none if they were forward.

So, while the ship slept, I in my ignorance sat on the grating in the shadow of the poop wetting my toes in the St Lawrence River, hoping to catch another big fish, bigger than the lavatory one! Reclining in this quiet secluded retreat I mused on this and that and watched the depths. In the shadow of the counter stern the water was clear of sun reflection and I could see far down beyond the heel of the rudder to a greenish nothingness.

Sometimes I could see a fish moving effortlessly against the current of the stream while at times I saw a bright silver flash as the afternoon sun caught the scales of a fish turning far below the surface. I would have liked to be down there, to see the various species of fish and the rockstrewn landscape of the sandy bottom as I imagined it to be. But I thought that it would be too deep for me to swim down and look at these marvels.

At the time, I had no idea that I would subsequently become a deep diver and would work aboard and inside the war-torn wrecks of ships lying on the bottom of the sea, so I contented myself with an acute examination of the green grass growing on the outside of *Lancing*'s iron hull. As I sat there with the fishing line lying over my index finger and in partial boredom jerked the line towards myself from time to time, as I had been instructed by my shipmates, I studied the weed growing below the waterline. A green growth which moved uniformly as the vagaries of the current caused it to undulate and appear alive. One moment it would look like a coat of thick paint with faint, longitudinal black lines weaving through it. Then a gust of wind aloft in the rigging or a slowing of the current of the stream would cause the ship to swing slightly and the weed would open out like the close-cropped hair of a drowned boy.

As I sat there doing nothing but jerk my wrist, my eyes grew heavy with lack of concentration while my body began to sway backwards and forwards gently. Later, this was explained to me by Dr MacColl. I was in danger of becoming mesmerized by the hot, glinting sun's reflection on the moving water and the sight of the far green depths.

Failing in my fishing and feeling the urgent need for sleep I coiled the line and hanging it in the fore rigging to dry entered the quiet and somnolent fo'c'sle and standing on my seachest eyed my bunk and slowly rolled into it.

Each night when the French-Canadians returned ashore in the empty scows or the work-boat, we boys and some of the able seamen raided the barrels of biscuits and molasses. It was a change from ship's food, good as that was.

I was introduced to chewing-tobacco. First the longshoremen brought it aboard since they were not permitted to smoke in the hold, though several times I saw them light up cigarettes and thin cigars called 'stogies'. Many of the able seamen chewed while at the wheel. The North American chewing tobacco was specially made for the purpose and contained molasses. Some called it 'molasses-kite' and it was so mild that it actually tasted like tobacco. The saliva could be swallowed with no ill effects. It was made up in cakes about three by two-and-a-half inches and a quarter-inch thick. It had a little tin heart fixed to one side by metal spikes, as a trade mark. We used to lay the heart, spikes upwards, on a seachest or bench just as a shipmate was lowering his backside down. I did not fancy chewing but did so out of bravado sometimes, especially when I had a lee wheel and was learning to steer, but I always missed the spitoon. Lack of sufficient power, I suppose.

Slowly the cargo rose in the hold, until it reached the level of the 'tweendeck beams. By this time I was heartily sick of stowing cargo and longed for the ship to put to sea so that we could return again to interesting work aloft and around the decks. I envied the Sailmaker who sat on his bench in the poop alleyway sewing sails, splicing and sewing the roping to them while we were gasping and sweating down in the dusty hold which now smelled so pleasantly of sawn lumber.

The Danish Carpenter had lost no time in going ashore and it was strange to see him again, dressed in his shore clothes and with a bigger canvas seabag on his shoulder than he first came aboard with, marching down the accommodation ladder behind the Captain to board the motor yacht which transported them to Matane, the day after our arrival, the Captain to 'enter' the ship at the Customs House and the former to return to the place of his adoption. Chips was a man who was not very popular, chiefly because he never missed an opportunity in conversation, to boast of the big money he had earned, as a 'tradesman', but like all big money earners he could only talk about it when he had nothing.

The Carpenter's successor was none other than 'mine enemy', the Finn! Several of the able seamen had been offered the job and had refused it, but he grasped the opportunity and withdrew from our midst, to my great delight and the satisfaction of most of my shipmates who considered him too unpredictable to be comfortable to live with.

At last came the day when the beams were shipped in the hatch coamings and we filled the space between with bundles and hundreds of birch sticks hammered into every crevice. As we did this, the bundles on each side moved even closer to the others which we had thought were already tightly packed. The hatch covers were put into place and caulked by the new carpenter and two of the able seamen, then the three tarpaulins were drawn over the hatch and secured, then battened down as each hatchway finished loading one by one.

The cargo gear was unrove, blocks and wires sent down and the dollies dismantled. The longshoremen departed, abandoning the biscuit and mollasses barrels with their depleted contents; these we stowed in the Bo'sun's locker to be clear of the chain cable. The cockbilled yards were squared, lifts and topsail sheets shackled on, then after a good wash-down of decks while the good-byes were being said in the after cabin, we rigged the chain messenger from the windlass to the steam winch at the main hatch.

In due course the shore people boarded the yacht and Mr Larsen, the Chief Mate, summoned us to pass two light tow-ropes to the motor yacht and the work-boat respectively which now lay close under the bows moving slowly ahead against the current of the river. There was a shout from the Second Mate of 'hand to the wheel' and someone detached himself and moved aft.

The steam winch started and with a rattling and jumping of the chain-messenger the windlass commenced to turn over, bringing the anchor cable aboard as the chain was hove short. With the cable nearly up and down we passed the two light tow-ropes out of both towing hawse-pipes, down to the small motor vessels where they were made fast. It would be interesting now to know how and where they were made fast for I do not remember.

The motor yacht had a deck-load of the women and girls to whom I had been presented and who now became the subjects of various lewd speculations arising between my shipmates.

I was sent out on the bowsprit to cast the gaskets off the jib and fore topmast staysail and from my vantage point I had an excellent view of the ladies—and they of me, so I showed off, climbing and skipping around the big spar, performing feats of agility. Finally, coiling the gaskets with wide dramatic sweeps of my arms while standing on the wire footrope and bowsprit guy, I watched the starboard anchor slowly appear above the surface and rise up, dripping and slimy, towards the hawse-pipes.

I was called in off the spar by the Bo'sun and my performance brought to a close as the headsails were hoisted up the stays and sheeted home, in order to assist the small motor boats to swing the ship's head to starboard. Lower topsails were loosed and sheeted home to the hauling cries of the seamen and the shuffling scrape of booted feet as the small tugs cast off the tow-ropes and we ran them aboard half-way along the main deck, while the heavy upper topsail yards crept steadily up the masts with the halliards round the drum-ends of the steam winches.

Sail after sail was set in fairly rapid succession and when the yards were braced for a fair wind, the motor boats which had circled us gave a last blast of their tinny whistles and the raucous rasp of a hand klaxon and turned away with much waving of hands and calls of, *'Bon voyage, mon Capitaine! Bon voyage, mes amis! Au revoir, matelots!'* A voice at the braces complained loudly. 'What the hell have *they* got to be so bloody pleased about? We don't even know 'em. We ain't never bin ashore!' The answer was given by the Sailmaker. 'That's *why* they're happy!'

It was a bitter disappointment to me that I had not found an opportunity to go ashore, actually walk on Canada. I had asked my shipmates why we were not allowed ashore and I was informed that it was because a Bond of 1,000 dollars would have to be posted to cover the desertion of each man, so if four men jumped ship the owners would forfeit 4,000 dollars. If a deserter was caught and brought back aboard the Owners would recover the remainder of their 4,000, less the expenses incurred in catching, feeding and transporting the delinquent.

Scandinavians, like the Scots and Irish, are incurable emigrants. At least one third of the seamen in *Lancing* had 'jumped' some ship and worked ashore in the U.S.A., Canada, Australia, New Zealand and South America at some time, judging by their reminiscences.

I had no intention of deserting the ship but I did propose that I could hide in one of the scows as it returned empty in the evening, and return aboard in the morning in a full one. I argued that I could walk around the town and find a place to sleep on the beach when it was dark. They succeeded in dissuading me by pointing out that the police would pick me up as soon as they saw me because my clothes were different from that of the local inhabitants and I did not speak French. I had no Canadian or American money with which to buy a meal, or even a cup of coffee. Someone pointed out, 'He wouldn't need money, he could bum his eats!' It was explained to me that this was just begging, going from back door to back door and asking for a 'handout' also referred to as 'battering castles!' I did not think much of that idea.

This fo'c'sle discussion opened up a subject in which some of my shipmates were well versed. I gathered that a few of them had travelled from coast to coast in the United States in and under box and flat cars on the railroads as hobos and that they had also passed a few weeks in various jails because they could not produce money or proof of a permanent address.

I was interested at the time to hear all this and had no idea that in later years I too would experience a little of this way of life that they described, in Australia and Canada, but only for short periods between jobs. There was no dole in those countries when I worked in them. When a man became unemployed there he had to scratch around quickly and find another job. Landlords had a habit of slinging you into the street if you were only a week in arrears with the rent. But in my case I did not have to desert a ship. I paid off a small delivery job in Sydney and it was a case of dead man's shoes when I signed on a Canadian steamer in Liverpool and paid off in Vancouver.

CHAPTER THIRTEEN

Homeward bound before the Westerlies

The ship suffered from light airs in the Gulf of St Lawrence but once clear of the coast of Newfoundland she picked up the Westerlies and went away like a train! We were homeward bound and mighty glad to be quit of the soul-drenching work in the hold, to be clear of the land and with a modest pay-day facing us. Bound away to the eastward across the Western Ocean, our hearts were glad and full of hope at the imagined prospects awaiting us ashore. We quickly settled into the routine of watch and watch, picking up the threads of our seagoing life again. Larvik was back with us after his 16 easy nights as ship's watchman. To me his advent was strange.

The empty bunk under Pelle's was a pleasant reminder of the grim and bitter experience when I suffered at the hands of the young Finnish seaman. Not unnaturally I have always resented actions or words directed against myself which I knew to be unjust. The man had, for no reason that I could understand, singled me out as the victim of his hatred, so it was not surprising that he had aroused a similar and perhaps stronger antipathy towards himself. Had he not obtained the vacant carpenter's berth and shifted out of the fo'c'sle, he and I were heading for serious trouble for I was conscious of a resolution forming in my mind, that the next time he picked on me as his personal punchbag, I would let him have it with whatever weapon I could lay my hands on, and damn the consequences!

At the time I could not contemplate a further 30 or 40 days at sea, during which I would be battered by the fists of a half-witted seaman at any time he chose to administer his form of fo'c'sle discipline for the most trivial reason. It never occurred to me to complain to the Captain, through the Second Mate. I have no doubt now that the bullying which I was undergoing at odd times would have been brought to a sudden stop! But I had been brought up in the schoolboy tradition of never, under any circumstances, telling tales to gain an advantage. So I suffered.

Happily it was the big Russian and not me, who put the final damper on the violence of the Finn. Shortly before we picked up the coast of Labrador when outward bound, I had entered the fo'c'sle and was suddenly confronted with the young Finn. He mouthed and screamed what sounded like threats, into my face and stabbed the stem of a pipe towards my eyes, which I easily evaded. I had no idea what had unleashed his fury but it appeared that one of his socks was missing and seeing me wipe a paint brush with a piece of green material which I then threw over the side, he had assumed from its colour that it was his lost sock.

Again he stabbed at my face with the stem of the pipe but I ducked, then suddenly the pipe hit the deck and shattered into fragments. The Russian had intervened and knocked it flying. Then he started on the Finn. He did not hit him but he cursed and raved, shouted and banged the table and a bunkboard with his big fists, using language that the other understood. I could see from his actions that he was intervening on my behalf and suddenly I was happy and at peace with the world and all men. The Russian's huge arm pointed in my direction while a single finger of his other hand poked the chest of the Finn repeatedly, while he continued to shout, rave and stamp his big feet.

For a minute or two I thought that the Finn was not going to take this public dressing-down and I hoped that the pair of them would start fighting, but the younger man backed slowly away and was obviously trying to justify himself, as with out-flung arms he appealed to the other seamen in the fo'c'sle.

Finally, as the din died down, Larvik and the Farmer instituted a search. They delved into seaboots, looked under bunks and throwing aside the blankets in the Finn's bunk they found the missing sock! I was vindicated. I felt like a martyred saint. From that moment the Finn never laid a finger on me. But I was never completely sure that the peace was but an armistice.

At the anchorage one evening, I was talking to the Farmer and I brought up the matter of the Finn's sock.

'I thought they would start fighting!' I said.

'No,' he replied, 'they would not fight, for if the big feller got his hands to work on the Finn, he could strangle him or break his back, an' the Finn knows it. So, if it came to a scrap, the Finn would use his knife and the Russian would have to use his too. These men from far up north don' fight like us. Not while they have a knife handy!'

He elaborated. 'They both know that a fight once started, will end up as a carving session, so they hold off as long as they can, see?' I saw. And I remembered his words in later years when I saw the same thing happen time after time when tempers flared between men of races to whom the knife is their natural weapon, particularly between Arabs. What appeared to be screaming timidity was in reality, self-control under duress.

The last personal contact that I had with the Finn after the incident of the sock was when he played a joke on me. It was, I think, his way of expressing his regret before a crowded fo'c'sle. He handed me the front cover page of a glossy magazine saying that he would show me a 'good trick!'

On his repeated instructions I folded the single page, first in half, then in half again, and so on. Using all the strength of my fingers I had reduced the page to the size of a five shilling piece. Then he told me to open it out. When I unfolded the much-creased page and exhibited it, he instructed me to roll it into a ball, crush it violently between the palms of my hands—and once more open it out. When I had gone through all this performance, the former stiff and glossy paper resembled a soft piece of rag. On request I handed it back and he left his seat and went to leave the fo'c'sle; quickly I asked him where the 'trick' was. He replied that it lay in getting someone else to do the hard work of rendering an unfit piece of paper fit for use in the lavatory! With that simple explanation he departed, howling with laughter.

Another hoary old trick which was played on me, early in the voyage, was started off by one of the elderly able seamen who told me to go and ask the Sailmaker for the 'manavellins'. This, I was informed by some of the seamen who had sailed in steamers, was also known as the 'black pan'. It was the un-consumed food from the cabin table, given to the firemen as extras, along with their own dinner or supper, when they came off watch at 2000.

To an ever-hungry boy this sounded fine, so I went in search of the Sailmaker. He knew all about it, but said I would have to ask the Carpenter. Chips said that I would have to ask the Bo'sun. He sent me to the Second Mate who was off watch and reading a book in the officers' messroom. He grinned and said that he thought that the Steward had already taken it forward and given it to the Donkeyman, so I had better apply to the latter for my share!

On my way forward along the main deck towards the fo'c'sle, the memory of the officer's grin awakened suspicion: I was being directed to too many people. It dawned on me that this was working out like a leg-pull. I hoped that it was not, and that 'manavellins' did exist and that I would get my share of them. But I had grave doubts now!

I knew all about green oil for the starboard sidelight and red oil for the port one and about the key of the keelson to wind the chronometer. And, of course, being sent with a bucket to the Donkeyman for 'a bucketful of blue steam please' and having the valve pointed out and told, 'Fill 'er up yerself!'

I had been well-briefed on these hoary old gags before I went to sea but manavellins was new to me. However, I later learned that they did, in fact, exist, but not in *Lancing*. Her afterguard were a hungry lot and there were no manavellins left for the boys. I would have to get along as best I could on sweet soup, *fiskeballas*, salthorse, burgoo, *lobscouse*, bread an' yam and the delicious, delectable pea soup.

When the ship picked up the strong westerly winds she sailed free on a north-easterly course and went swinging along in fine style. I noticed a change in her motion now, she was steadier and did not roll so quickly, due to the weight of her cargo, but she was wetter. Indeed, she had the reputation of being a wet ship and she was also known as a killer. Seamen said that she lost a man a voyage! I do know that she lost a former Captain over the side on a passage to Montevideo.

Small seas broke aboard through the lee scuppers and wash-ports, cascading across the decks and around the hatches and winches as she rolled to windward but before the creaming rushing water could escape, the ship would give a majestic lee roll and the water would rush back to where it had entered and build up in the lee scuppers as it made its way overboard again.

It was just such a time as this, that I have retained a vivid mental picture of the master of the ship, Captain P. Th. Pedersen. There had been some trouble forward and both Mates and the two watches were on the fo'c'sle-head. There was a heated argument about something to do with the chain lashings on the anchors having worked loose and I was standing near the starboard fore rigging on the main deck when I saw the Captain coming towards me along the waist. He was as usual dressed in an ordinary civilian suit of a dark colour. The jacket was open and flapping in the wind. He wore no waistcoat or collar or tie but a collar-stud fastened the neckband of his striped shirt. On his head was a cloth cap while his feet were encased by large, green woollen carpet slippers.

He walked slowly and with great dignity, arms loosely hanging, but what fixed my attention was the fact that a small sea had broken aboard as he came off the poop and was rushing from side to side as the vessel rolled. The water would reach to his knees one minute and be gone the next but he continued on his way forward, quite regardless of the cold discomfort swirling about his legs with each roll, perfectly calm and undisturbed. A shipmaster, master of his ship and all situations arising!

Naturally I did not know such an aloof personage as the Captain. My meetings ashore with him could hardly be called social and I did not have the experience to judge of his ability as a seaman but from what was said of him by the foremast hands, he was a fine seaman and a just man, their only criticism of him was that he hung on to the canvas too long for comfort—our comfort! It was hard and brutal work aloft when the sails had to be taken in in a gale of wind! Of course we growled at the time, but as the saying is, 'growl ye may, but go ye must!' In our hearts I think that we were all a bit proud of his ability and judgement as a sail-carrier.

Our dog-watch concerts in the fo'c'sle in fine weather out on the main hatch were, aside from heated arguments on ships and seamanship, the highlights of our existence. We all enjoyed them. They usually arose spontaneously, perhaps because the musician who happened to be playing the accordion broke into a jig or a polka. Then the feet would tap, heads would nod in time, the blade of a sheath-knife would start to drum on a sea-chest or a tin plate, out would come the Jew's-harp and two spoons would make their clacking felt in the blood!

The favourite melody for this, was called *The Hamburger*. A couple of massive able seamen would lift their bottoms off sea-chests, bow politely to two others and, 'Request the pleasure of this dance, Madam.' The seated ones would flap imaginary fans agitatedly, looking upwards coyly, then with little feminine gestures much exaggerated, would rise up and face their partners. Seldom did they dance in each others arms except when waltzing, and then they just clasped hands, because the form of their dances usually followed that of a wild Irish jig or Scottish square dance.

Not more than three couples could move around at one time, even when the table was wedged up under the deck-head, and then the 'wallflowers' had to keep their feet out of harm's way by drawing them on top of the seachests, otherwise the dancers would have made mincemeat out of them.

Our pleasures were simple and do-it-yourself, but they quickened the blood in the veins, caused hilarity and cheerfulness and started the night watches off with good-humoured memories. As often happened, an old and loved folk-melody would be played and awake a sentimental longing for another kind of life; for green fields, lichen-covered rocks, wood smoke and pine forests, or for the quiet, warm, lamp-lit peace of a kitchen fireside with a snowstorm blowing outside the window and a soft downy bed with a girl in it.

Much of the thoughts of a seaman at sea are concerned with the delights and the comforts of the land and a great deal of his conversation follows this pattern. When ashore he talks about ships and seafaring and wild nights in strange ports. That rarity, the seaman with a settled home ashore, usually has pictures of ships on the walls and a model of a barque behind the glass fan-light over the front door, while the same man afloat prefers views of grazing animals in lush meadows and the beauty of a mountain landscape or a nude woman.

During the voyage I had been invited by the able seamen to, 'come aft and learn to steer a ship'. I was informed that the proper procedure was for me to ask permission of the officer on watch to be allowed to take a lee wheel. After much consideration and hesitation, because I then believed that steering a ship was the summit of seamanship, I asked permission of the Chief Mate during a Sunday afternoon in my precious watch below. This was readily granted and I entered the wheel-house and mounted the two steps to the lee side of the big wheel.

I do not remember who the helmsman was but one thing I do know, I did not know one point of the compass from another. Later, I was given a rough pencilled diagram of a mariner's compass by Blackbeard but as the cardinal points were marked in Norwegian letters, this caused some confusion a year or so later when I was faced with an English compass which I had mentally to translate, using the well-marked North as the basis of research.

However, I poised myself at the side of the wheel and grasped the spokes in a seamanlike manner. The helmsman on the other side informed me that he was steering a compass course as the wind was free. I found the wheel spokes too large for my hands and, without realizing why, that the wheel turned easily. I had overlooked the fact that the strength exerted was that of the helmsman and not mine.

The two hatches on the fore corners of the wheelhouse deckhead were open and from time to time the shadow of the old Chief Mate would fall across us and I was conscious that we were under observation as he walked quietly fore and aft on the poop.

I remained about an hour at the wheel and learned practically nothing about steering but I got the feel of it. Next time I asked the big Russian if he would mind if I took a lee wheel with him. He was perfectly willing, so during the dog-watch one evening I obtained the consent of the Second Mate and again entered the holy centre of activity.

This time the ship was sailing 'by the wind' or as close to the wind as it was possible to go without getting the sails aback. The weather leech of the jigger royal was shivering and shaking while the remainder of the sail was full of wind. Under the tuition of the Russian, on this and other occasions, I really learned to steer a sailing ship. He gave me work to do! He did not allow me to be an automatic stooge on the lee side of the wheel, passing the spokes through my hands with no real effort on my part. Instead, he called me over to the weather side and made me steer the ship under his direction while he stood close behind me and helped turn the big six-foot, ten-spoked wheel and resisted the violent kick of it as the wind in the sails acted against the pressure of the water on the rudder blade.

He showed me how to bring the ship up close to the wind and hold it there. He told me that the royal yards were braced up sharper than the other yards below them, as an indication to the helmsman that the ship would point no higher once the weather leech of the royal started shivering from lack of wind pressure. So long as this side of the sail was trembling and flapping, all was well. The vessel was being correctly steered. But if the royals became full of wind or conversely, were empty of wind and flapping from the weather yard-arm to the lee clew and the t'gallant leech below started flapping too, then look out for a spot of bother from the officer on watch! Or a loud roar from the Captain.

Later in the fo'c'sle he showed me how to make corkscrew sennit with rope-yarns and pointed out that the yards were always braced in a similar fashion, even when the wind was fair. The lower yards were 'freer' than those above them, so that the officer on watch would have visual and audible warning when the ship was running too far to leeward or pointing too high into the wind and was in danger of going aback, so bringing the wind on the front of the sails when a dangerous situation could arise, maybe leading to the dismasting of the vessel or its total loss, depending on the force of the wind, the run of the seas and the loading.

The able seamen were a mine of information regarding sea-manship, particularly rigging. I learned some small facts from most of them. Later, when I was a cadet in steamers I learned practically nothing, except what I swotted up in books or, when I had mastered sufficient Urdu or Hindustani, from the Lascar crews. Cadets seemed to be just a form of cheap labour and no one was encouraged to teach us anything but polishing brass, cleaning windows and ports, handling signal flags and being polite to passengers.

I think that the apprenticeship system is too constrictive in its effects. While it offers social privilege it dampens efficiency, for the intake of officers from the fo'c'sle is very low. Amongst many serving officers that I have sailed with, seamanship was pushed into second place and the science of navigation was given pre-eminence. I had seen one or two of these brilliant minds come to total grief in an emergency and it was not due to them that the results were not disaster.

Under the apprenticeship system, boys are put in authority over other boys. This is to my mind a bad practice, for most of their knowledge has to come from their books while the senior cadets hobnob with the officers instead of bending their energies to advance the knowledge of their juniors in practical ways. Many of the officers encourage this and the senior cadets become blue-eyed boys who are only too willing to work out an officer's star sights while he dozes in the moon shadow of the bridge awning. So, decade after decade, men are produced who are navigators *par excellence* and have a wide theoretical knowledge of the art of seamanship and a practical knowledge of boat sailing on lagoons which fit them to command liners and super ships in all seas in the worst of weather conditions.

Parents want their sons to go to sea as gentlemen, brassbound and all. But many of the upper-income Scandinavian parents were not afraid to let their sons sign on as deck boys and sail in the fo'c'sles of vessels. They worked in ships and steamers for at least one long voyage covering perhaps a year, or even more, then returned home having learned a language and experienced the companionship of skilled men instead of youths of similar age. After this they would carry on their studies for a profession or enter their fathers' business. Mix boys with men and an adult state of mind is produced much more rapidly than is the case when boys spend formative year after year slowly evolving among their own contemporaries.

* * *

The seamen in *Lancing* did something which I have seldom seen other seamen do, they re-proofed their own oilskins. Of course British seamen give an oilskin a coat of oil, but they never make a thorough job of it. They simply brush it on over the old coat. I watched the Russian and others work for days over their oilskin suits. They steeped and scrubbed them in strong, hot soda-water to which was added some caustic. When all the oil was removed and they got down to the cloth, it was dried, then progressively given three or four coats of oil. They all went to a great deal of trouble and the results justified the work.

The young Finn brought out from the bottom of his seachest a suit that had never had a coat of oil. It was a pale grey colour and I think that it was calico material. I have no idea where such garments were sold, at a guess perhaps France or Holland. Some ship-chandlers presumably sold the made-up suit, complete with buttons and leather reinforcement, and left it to the purchaser to finish the job.

Those who wanted yellow suits simply painted on the oil but if black suits were preferred then a little black paint was added to the mixture. All had their own ideas for proofing, some said this and some said that, but the differences were slight. Except for one original who claimed that the oil-wet suits should not be hung up to dry as half the oil dripped away. They should be rolled up tight and left to soak. Nobody listened to his advice and he did not attempt to proof his own oilskins. For a couple of weeks it was impossible to move freely under the fo'c'sle-head for the ghostly shapes of oilskins slung on broomshafts like scarecrows. They were never permitted to dry in the sun, only in the cool shadows.

Another thing that the seamen were very particular about was their seaboots. In fine weather they frequently examined their condition and rubbed tallow into the leather and beeswax into the sewn seams. Mine had become wrinkled around the ankles through over-use, so they advised me to fill them with fresh water and hang them up. This would stretch them and take the wrinkles out, soften the leather and prevent leaks.

In this ship I found to my surprise that the Scandinavian people were patriotic when any question of their countries' superiority arose. The first occasion that I had this brought to my attention was when I visited the ship in the company of Alan Blanner. We were standing beside the taffrail and the big ensign was hanging down in limp folds from the staff. I touched the flag and seeing the red, white and blue colours mixed in the folds, I, in my youthful thoughtless ignorance, said something about it being 'a nice clean Union Jack'. Alan rounded on me in a flash and said hotly, 'It's not a Union Jack, you ass,' adding proudly, 'It's the flag of Norway!' And he was a Dane. I became more of a diplomat after that.

The second occasion was when I was at sea in the ship. I think it was about the third night out from Ardrossan and some order had been misinterpreted and the wrong sheet had been slacked away, or something like that. I had finished my particular job of coiling down the gear and when I returned to the fo'c'sle I found the able seamen grouped round the table talking to the Second Mate. His uniform cap and long oilskin coat were wet with rain and it dripped from his nose and cap. Leaning over the table with the knuckles of his fists resting on the scrubbed boards he was listening to their explanations.

As I watched and listened I heard the Farmer say to him, 'Look, Mister, everybody aboard here understands and speaks English so why not give the orders in that language, then there wouldn't be this sort of balls-up?' The Second Mate thumped the table hard with both fists, straightened and answered loudly *in English*, vehemently, 'This is a Norwegian ship and all commands will be given in the Norwegian language!' Without further discussion he turned and left the fo'c'sle.

Until I realized that foreigners had also been patriotically educated I was under the impression that Great Britain was the only country in the world that mattered to anyone. I had been taught, of course, that banking, coal, iron, ships and machinery were the basis of our greatness and that all foreigners were inferior to us, intellectually and physically! I had also been informed through the medium of the Press, that 'one Britisher was the equal of half-a-dozen foreigners!'

If that were true, I could lick and defeat any three of my shipmates, since by these odds I was only half the size and weight of six. Yet here I was, battered by a half-witted Finnish seaman and slapped around by a Norwegian Second Mate and there was nothing I could do about it. Something was very wrong with the educational system somewhere! Gradually it grew on me that national groupings are only a product of mankind, just like coal, iron and machinery. And they are sold across the counter by the same means—advertising. A form of controlled boasting.

CHAPTER FOURTEEN

Through Breaking Seas at 14 Knots

I have a vivid memory of the one and only time in *Lancing* that I received an issue of spirits. It happened when the ship encountered the storm on her westward passage and we had been aloft for hours, shortening down and finally heaving-to the vessel.

With the words, 'That'll do the watches. Watch on deck keep handy!' we were dismissed and all hands wearily entered the fo'c'sle for a smoke and a rest. Before we had time to take the lashings off our oilskins, the Bo'sun appeared at the doorway, his face wreathed in smiles. He said something in Norwegian which brought instant alertness and answering smiles to many faces and a quick translation of 'Splice the mainbrace!'

We all trooped aft in the lee of the weather bulwarks, along the heaving, wind-swept decks, heedless of the flying spray sweeping the waist and assembled outside the cabin doorway, sheltered a little by the overhanging ladder-platform. Wearing his ceremonial white jacket the Steward was braced just inside the doorway, holding a bottle of Red Label whisky in one hand and a large wineglass in the other. He managed to pour a generous tot without spilling a drop, in spite of the wild lurches and pitching of the ship, and to each man he said as he finished pouring nearly a glassful, 'This is with the good wishes of Mr Martin!'

When it came my turn and I presented myself before him with hand delicately poised to receive the glass, he looked at my face and hesitated, saying something about 'boys', and 'too young!' But a couple of the able seamen overruled his scruples. 'Give the boy his drink—entitled to it—worked with all of us— needs it now—do him good!' So the Steward carefully poured

my tot into the glass, a smaller amount than that given to the
other seamen but still a generous 'two fingers', men's fingers,
not mine. There was another full bottle lying on the deck of the
alleyway which the Steward pinned down with one foot, so that
it would not slide about and be broken.

I had watched the clear amber spirit rising in the glass and as
I raised it to my mouth and licked the salt off my lips the sweet
and pleasant aromatic scent rose around my face. I said a
hurried 'Tak—Skol!' and downed the lot in one quick gulp,
handing back the glass. Licking my lips and wiping them with
the back of my hand as I had seen the others do, I offered my
thanks to the Steward for Mr Martin's generosity and with a
rolling gait I ambled forward to the fo'c'sle to eat my food and
await the onset of intoxication, which I was certain would follow!

For a minute or two nothing happened, but gradually as I
sat on my seachest a warmth flowered in my stomach, spreading
upwards and outwards, reaching into my arms and legs and
down into my hands and feet. I had a wonderful feeling of
weightlessness, of being light, relaxed and very comfortable so I
just sat where I was and basked in the benign influence of
alcoholic contentment, too satisfied to divest myself of my
oilskins.

I belched! One of the crowd of men indicated me with outstretched thumb. 'Yack's a boozer now!' This statement started
the good-natured kidding. 'You're learnin' to be a sailor—
fast!' Then I was informed that before I could be a real seaman
I would have to cultivate certain pleasant vices, such as growing
rope-yarns on my chest instead of hair. Drink myself unconscious when I paid off a ship. Round the Horn in sail, and
master four women in one night! 'Then ye can call yerself a real
sailor!'

I laughed at the rope-yarn theory but gave the others some
small consideration. I figured that it should be fairly easy to get
drunk once in a while. But only on whisky! And rounding the
Horn in sail? Well that was bound to happen to me, sooner or
later. If not in this ship, then some other. 'Four women?' I
asked. 'Why four? One would be enough!' They replied, 'But
think of the fun ye could 'ave.'

*   *   *

Remembering the first time that I was given the job of cleaning and polishing the big brass bell atop the fo'c'sle house, I noticed another name engraved on it instead of *Lancing*. I called down to Larvik on the main deck, who explained that it was her name when she was a steamer under the French flag. It was traced out in beautiful script, each letter separate and I am certain that there was a two-letter prefix to the *Pereire* though there is no historical evidence of this in any surviving documents. The name faced forward not aft, as is customary, the bell having been turned round.

*   *   *

It was in the fo'c'sle of *Lancing* that I first heard about the German commander, Kapitan Graf Felix von Luckner and his disguised raider, the auxiliary full-rigged ship *Seeadler*, ex *Pass of Balmaha*. This was some years before I read his book. Our seamen held him in great respect but they criticized the loss of his ship on a reef in the South Pacific while the vessel was at anchor. They maintained that it must have been due to carelessness, that the vessel should have been kept off the land, standing off and on, and that the stores could have been landed on the island with the ship's boats, without anchoring!

I was eager for details but my shipmates did not know very much beyond the bare outlines of this romantic war story. I asked what '*Graf*' meant. I was told, 'Same as your English Lord.' Some years later, in 1926, I saw Count von Luckner coming ashore from his ship, the four-masted steel schooner, *Vaterland*, which was fitted out as a trade exhibition ship to boost the sales of German industry throughout the world. This was in San Pedro, U.S.A.

I had been brought up to detest the German race and all their works, but to my surprise there was no apparent hatred of them in the minds of my shipmates. Doubtless the Scandinavian neutrality and the fact that all of them had been at sea for long periods had kept them free of the violent hate propaganda in the British press and American films. Yet German submarines freely sank neutral shipping without discrimination.

Within a year, I was in Hamburg and Bremerhaven and I found the Germans that I came in contact with to be decent, kindly folk, clean in their habits and homes and with no

158

hate in their hearts towards us. They kept that for politicians!

Once, in my wanderings around Bremerhaven I became lost, and I must have looked it, for a small boy of about eleven or twelve years of age asked me, in perfect English, if I was looking for the docks. I was in cadet's uniform. He not only directed me but walked nearly a mile so that I should not again become lost. I thought it strange that our hatred of everything German had stopped the teaching of the language in our schools, and yet the Germans had continued to teach English. This youngster had obviously been taught it throughout the War.

I grew to have a high regard for German shipbuilding, merchant seamen, the knowledge displayed of their subject by marine artists, and engineering designers.

*   *   *

During the course of my voyage in *Lancing*, I did some silly things unthinkingly. One night when coiling the gear on the pins after the change of watches, I heard the Second Mate, who was hidden in the darkness of the waist, shout out something that sounded to me like, 'All hands on deck!' Without hesitation I dashed into the fo'c'sle, thinking that some sudden emergency had arisen, and bawled out in great excitement, 'All hands on deck!'

Some of the seamen of the watch below, who had not yet turned in and were standing around in their long woollen underpants and sleeved undervests, looked towards me curiously. One old fellow pulled aside the towel-curtain of his bunk and sticking out his grey head asked, 'What the hell's wrong wi' *you*?' I was shocked by their immobility and lack of response to my news! One seaman stepped out on deck and returned to report that everything was 'All right outside.'

They demanded an explanation for my curious conduct and when I said that I was sure that the Second Mate had shouted for all hands to come on deck, they asked, 'What, in *English*?' When it dawned on me that no commands were given in my language I slunk out of the fo'c'sle in deep shame and embarrassment. My gut crawled at the thought of what would have happened to me had the watch below been sound asleep!

Another time I was on the look-out and it was a quiet moonless night with dark clouds low overhead and the flicker of lightning far beyond the horizon. The ship was running free with the wind over the starboard quarter and travelling at a speed of about seven or eight knots. She was sailing steadily with little movement and looking overside the bow wave, as the stem sliced the sea apart, was pale blue with phosphorescence. Walking slowly from side to side and avoiding the glare of the side-lights as I turned at the rails I looked aft and noticed a long glowing shape gliding through the water close to the lee side and nearly abeam of the mainhatch. I was instantly interested. This was a *big* fish! It did not act like a porpoise so I reached the conclusion that it must be a shark.

I kept it under observation for several minutes, trying to determine its exact shape and expecting it to alter course suddenly away from the ship and dive down into the depths. However, it seemed determined to stay with the vessel, so I hastily slid down the ladder handrails and looked for someone to share the excitement of this moment.

I slipped quietly and quickly into the fo'c'sle and there was Pelle standing on his seachest and rummaging in his bunk, looking for something, so I whispered urgently, 'Hey, Pelle, come out on deck quick and see the big shark alongside!' As we returned to the deck we encountered two other seamen of the watch and the four of us climbed up on to the rail and looked directly down on the monster of the deep!

There were angry growls then laughter, and one of the audience spoke disgustedly, 'Christ, that's the Cook's hammock!' The latter had unearthed a canvas hammock which he used for sleeping on deck in the tropics and this was his method of washing it, by towing it alongside. Fresh water was too precious to use for such a purpose in a sailing ship. I felt ashamed and retreated hurriedly to my deserted post on the fo'c'sle-head. I was mighty glad that I had not encountered the Bo'sun's Mate when I had abandoned the look-out, for a hard slap and a swift kick would have been administered summarily.

Under no circumstances was the look-out man permitted to leave his position unless ordered to do so. If he urgently wanted to attend the calls of nature he was supposed to stamp his foot heavily on the deck and by this means, summon a relief. But as this was not popular with the one summoned, it was never done. Instead we carried a bit of paper in a pocket and if necessary, climbed over the rail at the knight-heads, dropped down on to the triangular plate sheathing over the stem-head and hanging on to the foot-rope, projected our bottoms over the side, just as the sailors did in the ships of Elizabeth I.

It is not generally known, but that is the true purpose of the fancy gilded cagework round the bows of these ancient ships for they had no other type of such accommodation for the common mariner. The builders certainly did not put all that weight of timber round the bows merely as ornamentation, as a lot of artists appear to imagine. Surely the purpose is evident from the shape of the structure? These are the original 'heads'. I have since thought that it must have been quite a sight when one of these old ships was in port with a full crew confined aboard, in, say, Bristol, where the docks are in the centre of the city!

One sunlit but wild day when *Lancing* was sailing grandly before a strong north-west wind at $14\frac{1}{2}$ knots (a speed given to us by the man coming away from the wheel) the topmasts of a steamer were sighted ahead. Two hours later she was steaming abeam of us, under the lee and about half a cable's length away. Our ship was on the port tack under all plain sail with the wind about two or three points abaft the beam. The steamer appeared to be a German-built vessel of about 10,000 tons deadweight, a three-island type of cargo ship with a black hull, white superstructure and broad, yellow-painted funnel while her masts and derricks were ochre colour.

Watch below and watch on deck alike, crowded on to the fo'c'sle-head and the big Russian threw the coil of the fore topmast staysail sheet on to the deck and picking up the end he waved it in the air and flicked it over the side in the direction of the steamer, yelling at the top of his considerable lung power, 'Hey, Dutchy, want a tow?' His cry was taken up by most of us as we danced about waving our arms and laughing in triumphal excitement. Suddenly from the funnel of the steamer a plume of thick black smoke belched out and trailed downwind. This caused more hilarity amongst us, as it was taken as a sign that the steamer did not like being overtaken by a windjammer and was trying to raise more steam in order to keep up with us, since it was obvious that she could never get ahead again.

Some wag shouted, 'What's a' matter, broken down!' and in spite of the black smoke which soon thinned and disappeared, the steamer slowly and surely fell behind us followed by jocular hails from some of our men, 'We will report you all well!' The pantomime left little to the imagination too!

When the steamer was well astern and following in our wake, I remembered my box-camera completely forgotten in the excitement of the chase and overhauling. However, I brought it up on deck and obtained some photographs of my shipmates while the Russian took one of me which turned out to be an excellent photograph. I had them all stolen by boy thieves in Birkenhead some years later when my chest was broken open in a four-masted barque I was serving in. The steamer was hull-down about two hours later and we never saw her again.

Lancing drove on to the eastward, running before strong westerly winds and big wind-torn seas. Now that she was deep loaded the height of the wave-crests appeared much higher than they were when we had encountered the storm when beating to the westward, outward bound. And they were not content to stay where they were either. From time to time as the ship rolled, a sea would rear high above the rail and with a thunderous roar would come crashing aboard, sweeping over the hatches and winches and rushing across the decks in a spreading cataract of foam and black water. It spread quickly and lost depth as it found its way over the broad open main deck but sometimes it met another big sea pouring over the opposite rail and then the main deck would look like a picture of a sinking ship with the deck-houses, masts and lower rigging and perhaps a long section of one t'gallant rail showing above the surface of a sucking, boiling cauldron.

At such moments as this I was fascinated by the appearance of the sheets of the big courses. The ropes of the whip tore through the surface of the sea yards away from the ship and apparently unconnected to the hull. They threw up their own small waves and trailed a wake behind them while the straining sheet blocks dripped water and the clews of the sails were grey with wetness. But the ship would rise slowly and buoyantly to the hiss and gurgle of moving water, clanging wash-ports and sucking scuppers and the mass of water would quickly drain away overside as the winches reappeared, then the hatches, then the ringbolts, then the decks.

There might be a breathing space of ten minutes or half-an-hour between those broaching seas but before long over they would come again, and this continued for the best part of a week. Flooding decks made no difference to the work on deck for this went on regardless of weather. Sail handling and working the vessel was of paramount importance.

Many times we would be caught by a boarding sea when hauling on the braces or clewing up a sail. The Captain on the poop might shout or whistle a warning to the Second Mate who was with us on the main deck, probably slacking away the braces on one side of the ship while we hauled away on the other. Usually the warning would come too late, or would be unheard and with no time to scramble into the rigging for safety, all we could do was to hang on like grim death with aching arms and straining lungs and hope that we would not be too long submerged.

One dark night a big sea came aboard and swept the lot of us away from the fore braces. I thought my final fate had descended on me and I later heard that my shipmates had the same feeling. I did not know if I was still aboard the ship as I paddled about like a frightened dog in a whirlpool, trying to reach the surface wherever that was. I did not know if it was above or below me. The soles of my seaboots scraped against something which I think must have been the top of the main or mizzen hatch and I pushed hard and for a second or two managed to gulp some air into me, then I was rolled and twisted over and over, banged against something soft like a coil of rope, hit something hard then felt the iron plating sliding rapidly against my back and heels and for a moment I thought that it was the shell plating on the outside of the hull, that I was overboard and the ship was passing me!

My foot hit something hard, my other leg was caught and jammed while my body was wrenched sideways and I thought my legs were being broken, then my face felt air on it and suddenly the sea had left me. I was lying flat on my back on the deck under the poop overhang and under the starboard ladder but both feet were jammed between the side of the ladder and a boat-skid stanchion.

Just as I had painfully extricated myself the sea came back and flooded over me again and away I went, but this time the water was not very deep and I brought up in the scuppers of the port alleyway where I clung to the coils of the buntlines and clewlines hanging down above me. But the danger was past and we all managed to re-group and after a hasty count the Second Mate was heard reporting to the Captain that we were all still aboard and unhurt. Actually most of us were a mass of bumps and bruises but in a sailing ship a man is unhurt until he breaks a leg or an arm. Then came the job of tracing the snarled-up braces which had also been washed all over the ship, examining them for damage and finishing the job of trimming the yards, while we all moved heavily about in a soaked condition, the sea-water having penetrated our oilskins and drained into our seaboots.

In *Lancing*, there was a definite order of precedence when hauling on braces, sheets and halliards, etc. The able seamen were always nearest the block, then after them came the ordinary seamen while behind that lot were the deck boys. It was a sensible arrangement because it placed the stronger and bigger men where the height of the rope from the deck was greatest, but also there was the matter of pride in seniority. No able seaman would consider hauling on a line *behind* a deck boy!

My first experience of this came in Ardrossan prior to sailing. We were ordered to swing the yards and as soon as I saw where the men were making for, I joined them at the braces. Noticing a gap which would fit me, between two able seamen, I pushed in, laid hold of the rope and started hauling away with the others. A hard elbow struck my shoulder, two red-rimmed eyes glared down at me and a beer-laden breath blew into my face as the mouth of the man behind me growled, 'Hey, you, 'bout ship—get on the tail-end!' Another voice called out, 'Get forrard on the end of the line! No boys foreand 'ere!'

Sometimes in fine weather, the able seamen would play a trick on us. As the long line of men and boys hauled away at a single brace, our voices echoing the cries of the shantyman who was giving us the time, a man in the centre of the line would quickly double a portion of line as the slack came to him, by 'marrying' it and with the next swinging pull he would pass more line aft to his neighbour who would in turn pass the bight to his neighbour. When three men had the concealed double rope safely held they would wait for the next heave and then suddenly let the lot go. Everyone behind them would fall flat on their backs on the deck, having exerted all their weight and pulling power against three fathoms of slack rope!

Fine weather with strong fair winds gave the old four-masted full-rigged ship a magnificent push across the 2,500 miles of the North Atlantic. We commenced to smarten up the paintwork ready for her entry into port. First we washed the boats, deck-houses, ventilators and bulwark panels with 'soojie' which is a strong solution of washing soda and fresh water. This work has the effect of drying the skin of the hands, by removing temporarily the natural oils I suppose, because the skin turns leathery and milky in appearance, but it certainly improved the appearance of the painted surfaces.

We washed the soojie off with more fresh water and when the surface dried, out came the paint pots, rags and brushes and we painted the ship where we had first washed her clean.

Starting on the masts we gave them one coat. I remember painting the lower doublings. (Where one lower mast is joined above they form a double section.) Two able seamen nearby were discussing the ship and I heard one say, 'She's a heavy bastard!' Meaning that there were too few hands aboard for the work of such a big ship. This was news to me. I had thought that all sailing ships were 'proper workhouses'. It cheered me up to think that the work might be a lot lighter in other ships when I moved on.

The two seamen were using a teak-colour paint while I was applying white. I fancy I had been given the job of painting blocks and wire seizings and, of course, the cross-trees and spreaders above me. Anyhow, I was tired of using this sticky paint and voiced my feelings to the other two.

They informed me that I was fortunate. One said, 'My last ship had all the doublings white.' While the other man shocked me when he told of sailing in a barque which had a white hull and all the masts and yards were painted white too. 'She looked like a flamin' flour mill, going down channel!'

Later in the day, the Russian asked me if I planned to make another voyage in the ship. I replied, 'No, she's too heavy! I'm going to look for a lighter-working ship after this, perhaps a barque.' He gave me a look of smiling amusement, doubtless wondering what experience had given me the judgement of comparison, then warned me. 'Smaller ships, smaller crews.

More work for each man!' And I found that to be true too.
'But,' he added, 'you will learn more, more quickly, in a small
ship.' And how right he was!

With all painting aloft finished, we started at the taffrail aft
and with more white paint we did rails, ensign staff, ventilators,
boats, deck-houses, rigging screws and seizings, all white and
glossy. I think we also rubbed down the varnished lifebelt
box, steering and standard binnacles, skylight and cabin
companionway, with wet sharkskin and sand and canvas, but I
think the Mates did the varnishing.

We boys were given the job of polishing the scores of brass
bars fitted to the wheel-house trunk and the saloon skylight as
protection for the glass lights against careless feet or a swinging
boom tackle block or mooring rope.

We used bathbrick and oil on this brasswork and a messy
wearisome job it was, but when all the painting and polishing
was finished the poop was as smart as any well-kept yacht. The
lines coiled on the pins or flaked on the deck had a bleached and
work-worn look to them which, to my mind, did not detract
from the appearance of the whole, rather it added to it by
showing that this was a smart and powerful vessel that really
put to sea, and sailed!

During the work of painting ship, Larvik had unearthed the
uniform cap of some Naval seaman and had painted the word
LANCING across the front of it, for it had no ribbon, in large
white letters. He wore this with a challenging air and appreciated the amusement that it caused when he first appeared on
deck, for he was always full of fun. But the elements accepted
the challenge and he lost it shortly afterwards. It was swept off
his head by the wind as he was descending the rigging.

I also lost my only hat. It was a felt snapbrim, an old one of
my father's which I had 'borrowed' for the voyage. At least I
think it was an old one. I had moulded it into the shape, suitable to the adventure on which I had embarked, that of the
Royal Canadian North West Mounted Police, and I loved it!

I was overhauling lee buntlines when I felt it leave my head
and sadly I watched it sail away past the brace pendant and go
down and down with the wind, shrinking each heart-beat until
it landed softly in the turmoil of seas. With a saddened feeling
of loss my eyes followed as the ship swept onwards and I could no

longer distinguish it against the blue and the whites of the waves.

When I joined *Lancing* I was already as full of prejudices regarding sailing ships as it was possible to be. My reading and listening had seen to that. It took a long time and consumed a lot of varied experience for my belief in the 'steam-kettle theory' to shatter and fall apart. The talk that was handed down and found its way into print was:

'Steamer sailors, they ain't seamen, they're painter's mates an' handymen, deck-labourers! All they know is keepin' a lookout an' steerin' by compass. Twenty days at sea an' fresh meat and soft-tack (fresh bread) for ten of 'em!' Or, 'Ye can't go wrong in a bleedin' steamer, point 'em in any direction an' off they go. They ain't ships, they's only corned meat tins fitted with engines and an egg-beater under their arses! An' what starts 'em moving? Jist a blow of breath down a tube to the engine-room an' the pistons start goin' up an' down. Dead simple. No hard work at all!

'Now a sailing ship has no engines, so it's pure skill an' seamanship, an' *us seamen*, what makes them move around. We got no pistons goin' up an' down, or wheels turnin' round an' round shafts when an engineer pushes a couple o' levers. No, mate, we have good masts and yards, canvas, lines an' wind, an' with a bit o' grub an' water we takes our ships anywheres!'

Seamen who perpetuated these kind of yarns had little if any imagination. As well maintain that a windmill is not an engine. A sailing ship is herself an engine, drawing her motive power from natural sources and using applied science to reach her destination economically. *No pistons?* What are halliards but pistons moving in the vertical plane and governing the amount of power applied to the ship's motion. *No wheels turning round and round shafts?* Every one of the hundreds of blocks is equipped with from one to four wheels, called sheaves, which turn round shafts, called pins, and they all act as cranks, fulcrums, links and levers, and lift, lower, pull and turn while the wind supplies the push. This is all that the components of any engine does, while all require oiling, greasing and constant attention to their needs. The standing rigging forms the engine, and the running rigging is designed for the purpose of turning, twisting and adjusting the planes which convert air in free motion into direct hull-motion. The similarity between the *powered* vessel and the sailing ship is so obvious. In the former, the main engine is composed of a number of units each of which is an engine in itself with a single piston working within a cylinder. Each unit is independent, having its own services brought to it, such as fuel and electricity. Should a minor fault develop in one unit it can be isolated without impairing the normal running of the remainder.

The sailing ship has a similar layout with each mast performing as a single unit which is made up of standing and running rigging, yards and sails. In like manner to the internal combustion engine, one mast-unit can be isolated without seriously affecting the normal use of the others, whose sails will continue to function, providing balance is maintained. The services which activate the moving parts on each mast are the seamen and mates. *No engine?* It is the only type of engine whose human operators live and work inside it. Both types of motive power are started up in the same way, by means of a very small compressed air activated metal cylindrical instrument having two slotted orifices at right angles to each other and imprisoned within the cylinder, a hard pea.

A controversy has existed between seafarers for many, many years, 'Sail versus Power', but to my mind there is little basic difference between a marine diesel engine and the sail plan of a full-rigged ship. Both are propulsive mechanisms. Both are highly functional and successful. The basic design is similar. Both possess 'human appeal', power and beauty of line and form. So why should their devotees be separated? There is little to argue about.

I see no real division between deck and engine room, or automatic nobility of the sail-trained man. Service hardship is no guarantee of ability for I have been shipmates with a few duds in sailing vessels and a mass of fine and practical seamen in steamers. And one finds officers in both classes of vessels who, owing to good swotting ability and a retentive memory for text have succeeded in claiming the distinction of a bunk with drawers under it, instead of another bunk; but for the safety of the ship they would have been more usefully employed ashore as a bookies' 'tic-tac' man.

*   *   *

Word had gone round that we were approaching the coast of Scotland or Ireland, we did not know which, that the wood decks of the quarter alleyways on either side of the poop deck-house were to be holystoned! Pelle, Larvik and I had brought up two buckets filled with sand from the lazarette under the deck-house—with big ship's biscuits concealed in the sand. We emptied the sand into a sack, sharing our loot as we did so but the sight of the sudden appearance of the sand was too much for three of the seamen. Big Ed, the Farmer and the Russian flitted forward under the fo'c'sle-head where the holystones were stowed between the frames on both sides, close to the hawse pipes, and opening a lee port in the bow they dumped the lot into the sea! I do not now remember if trouble arose from this self-preservation sabotage but I think not. Because I happened to be there, they incriminated me by getting me to pass up to them some of the sandstone blocks while they pushed them through the porthole.

Holystoning is devil's drudgery! The deck planks are first wet down with seawater and sand sprinkled over them, and kept wet by additional sprinklings while the seamen kneel on the wet gritty deck and push with both hands, and draw a heavy block of sandstone up and down the grains of each plank for hours on end. One's hands, knees and toes become chafed and sore with the friction of the wet sand and the act of balancing against the movement of the vessel. I had had my share of this work shortly before our arrival at Cape Chat, so that I was not at all broken-hearted at seeing the lot passed through the porthole.

Steamers were frequent sights now. One evening just as the light was failing we saw a strange sight. To me it appeared to be a large cargo steamer towing a floating dry dock. They were on the horizon steering west and did not approach closer. The tow had the appearance of a big oblong box, high out of the water. The towing vessel was a 'three-island' steamer of about 10,000 deadweight tons and certainly had not the usual silhouette of deep sea tug.

The seamen were very interested and argued about it, some saying this and some that, but the Finnish carpenter was the one to elucidate. He said it was the steamship *Iroquois* towing the six-masted schooner *Navahoe*. Most of the watch agreed with him now that he had jogged their memories.

It appeared that for a year or two an experiment had been going on, based on cost presumably, of one tanker towing another across the Atlantic while both were fully loaded with bulk oil on the eastward passage; one was a steamer and the other a sailing vessel, schooner rigged. The sailing barge was *Navahoe* of 7,218 tons, built of steel by Harland & Wolf; her fore and aft sails were only for use if she broke adrift from the tug. The towropes were steel wire, seven inches in diameter and six hundred fathoms in length, connected to a towing-engine. She was fitted with ship-to-ship radio and carried an operator. I do not vouch for the fact that this is what we saw, but the seamen all agreed that it was. I could see no sign of one mast, let alone six, for my distant vision was as yet untrained, but I was convinced of the rightness of my shipmates' judgement since I had it borne in upon me that they had a very accurate knowledge of the commercial traffic upon the seas and oceans of the world.

One evening we saw a flashing shore light reflected on low cloud, far away off the starboard bow. The wind was still strong and the ship sailed grandly at about ten knots. The seamen were optimistic. 'To-morrow night we will be in!' and 'Ya, ya, pay-off Monday, fifteen days out from Cape Chat!' Every passage was spoken of in terms of days. Never of weeks or months.

All the crew had 'Channel fever' now and some were even starting to pack their seabags. I thought that I, too, would get ready to leave, so turned back my 'donkey's breakfast', now flattened in my bunk, as the straw filling having become brittle from much use had broken into small pieces, then I hauled my seabag from under it.

It is customary for the occupant of a top bunk to spread his seabag and any old piece of sailcloth over the boards of his bunk so as to prevent the straw dust from filtering through and down into the eyes, ears and mouth of the seaman in the lower bunk. My seabag was creased and soiled and smelled of dried hay so I thought that I would emulate the cook and tow the bag overside, saving myself the labour of scrubbing. I mentioned this to one of the senior seamen but he advised me to tow it ahead of the ship and not alongside, since there were probably '. . . barnacles like flamin' razors growin' below the waterline that'll cut yer bag t'ribbons!'

I had lost my washing a few days previously. Three half-cleaned grey shirts and some underwear had mysteriously disappeared from a line I had rigged between the anchor crane and the lower topsail sheets. I was informed that they had 'blown away during the night' but I suspected a Scottish deck boy in the port watch who had had a look-out on the night my washing 'went over the wall'. He was, I considered, rather a sneaky, toadying individual. My precious Waterman fountain pen, a birthday gift from my parents, vanished from my seachest about the same time.

I obtained a heaving line from the bo'sun's locker and, passing one end through all the brass eyelets in the mouth of my bag, formed a bowline. Climbing out to the end of the bowsprit I took a turn of the line and dropped the bag into the sea, watching it floating on the surface as the on-rushing stem approached. When the line tightened and the bag started to tow I eased away until it was rushing and skipping over the sea a fathom ahead of the knifing stem, then I made the line fast with many unnecessary hitches and returned inboard. Looking down over the bows I watched my bag plunging and twisting on the sea's surface, advancing ahead as the bows rose and swimming swiftly back as the stem plunged down, washing itself clean without any effort on my part.

The following morning at 4 a.m. I went on the look-out and when the seaman that I had relieved had departed to his bunk I looked over the bows. The bag had gone! Climbing over the rail and crouching under the bowsprit I scanned the sea anxiously while anger and suspicion mounted within me, but of seabag and heaving line there was no trace. Well, I thought, perhaps one of the look-out men had done me a good turn, taken it in and hung it up to dry somewhere, perhaps over the long-boat or maybe in the staysail netting, because the force of the wind had increased considerably since I had turned in at midnight.

I looked and searched in vain and as I resigned myself to my loss I noticed a dark shape high up against the gloomy clouds to leeward, swooping and diving in the wind like a great vampire bat.

A hasty investigation showed it to be attached to the bowsprit-end by a long line. It was my missing seabag held aloft by the upsurge of wind, probably from the curved plating of the weather bow. Until identified it had scared me for I had thought it to be a huge black noiseless bird!

Scrambling out along the bowsprit I brought bag and line inboard only to find that the force of the sea had punched out the bottom of the bag and only a third of it was still attached to the sides! I was not grateful in regaining my property and I cursed loudly and luridly. But it was my own fault. I should have lashed the neck securely and so prevented it from being forced open by the speed of the ship against the weight of water.

I had to stop awake in my next watch below and in the quiet of the Carpenter's Shop, re-stitch the bottom to the sides as best I could, with long 'homeward-bound' stitches.

CHAPTER FIFTEEN

Landfall, Pay Off and Home

Land was in clear sight when daylight came away and as the day wore on more of it appeared, stretched out along the port beam. The cables were hove out of the lockers, passed down through the unplugged and now draughty hawse-pipes and shackled on to the anchors which were hanging overside from each bow in their chain-releasing gear. A steam tug came out from the land but could not get near us owing to the speed of the ship, but it followed for about two hours before giving up the chase and turning shore-wards.

More land appeared to starboard in the late afternoon. The wind dropped as *Lancing* sailed under the lee of the land and her speed was now only about five or six knots. My seabag had been dried in the galley, thanks to the benevolent attitude of the Doctor who, taking pity on my plight, granted me this privilege. I hastily packed it with all my gear, which by this time was composed mostly of rags. Even my grey shore suit had been pressed into service and the inside of the trouser legs had long, puckered rips in the tweed material, put there by my sliding down back-stays in order to reach the deck quickly. The seat also had a great gash in it through which bare flesh showed.

I had been full of good intentions and had meant to repair my trousers as best I could, since my mother had given me plenty of sewing and darning materials wrapped in a cylindrical holdall, or tidy. This was shoved back into the seabag in the same state as when it was given to me.

I emptied the shelves of my bunk and the portbox of my few treasured possessions and resolved to leave my pin-ups where they were, for they were not the sort of art studies which would be appreciated by my mother. They were six cigarette cards of Mack Sennet Bathing Beauties who wore tight woollen bathing costumes, black silk stockings rolled down to below the knees and black court shoes with three-inch heels. Some had silk bandeaux round their foreheads while others preferred wide-brimmed, sloppy hats. All had very large black eyes and very small pouting lips and they were supposed to be sexy! Some carried parasols. I much preferred my others. They were drawings cut from *La Vie Parisienne*, of nude and semi-nude women in languorous attitudes and all had beautiful legs, slim ankles and small feet.

When at last my bag had been packed, I gazed down into my empty seachest whose interior was smooth and glossy, the white paint yellowed with age, the scent of its many old and compounded contents was to me, delicious and memory provoking. On the inside of the raised lid, within a large oval frame depicting an endless rope or grommet, was a barque of about 1,200 tons, sailing in a very blue and white sea. She was close-hauled on the starboard tack and had a white hull while her masts were teak-coloured. Every sail was set and drawing well while a bright Norwegian ensign flew from her spanker gaff. I wish now that I could remember her name. This appeared in black letters on her port bow and was repeated below the painter rope.

The painting was no work of art in the accepted sense but it had been executed with laborious care and attention to detail. It was an authentic reproduction of a sailing ship and as such it had achieved its object. It was *right* and it gave interest and pleasure and, no doubt, great satisfaction to the seaman-artist. It was of course unsigned. For a seaman to sign his picture would have been considered presumptuous and would have been taken as a sign of conceit, that the seaman considered himself an *artist*! So it was never done. The attitude was wrong, of course, but it existed. None of these paintings were produced for profit.

Some of the signed horrors which I have since looked upon in the windows of galleries would be incomprehensible to my former shipmates, just as they are to me now, and some of the pictures of alleged ships painted by 'marine artists' make me blush for their lack of knowledge of the subject depicted!

When my seabag was damaged I had considered the matter of taking home this seachest but when I spoke of it to the seamen they said, 'Ya, help yourself, but don' forget that a seachest needs two men to carry it.' So this project was reluctantly abandoned and the bag was repaired, after a fashion.

There were other paintings of ships on the inside of the lids of all other chests, bar one. Here the artist appeared to be obsessed with geometrical patterns involving circles, triangles and squares, all painted in basic colours which were confined within segments and diamonds, but it did have relativity and balance as a picture. It reminded me of fairground art. There were no steamers depicted anywhere, though some men had post-card photographs of steamers they had sailed in. There were also photos of schooners, barques and ships tacked on the inside lids in the form of a frame to the central picture. The photographs of the seamen's wives, families and parents were sacred and were never on display. They were hidden away in stained wallets and old paper envelopes or wrapped carefully in a clean piece of material like a silk handkerchief. All these were stowed carefully away in the small box-shelf which was common to the inside of every seachest, sometimes with a tiny, fitted lock to its lid. Perhaps wrapped with the photographs would be a caul. This is an envelope of skin or membrane which covers the head of some children at birth. Its possession is reputed to protect the owner from death by drowning. They could be bought in second-hand shops on any dock road and those that I have seen looked like dried and shrivelled bubble-gum in a brittle state.

Many of the photographs of the seamen's parents were printed on tin. Daguerreotypes which showed elderly men looking much older than their years, badly in need of a hair-cut and with big beards, uncomfortable collars and massive 'heirloom' watch-chains. The females of the family also appeared elderly and with sad, care-worn looks. Some expressions were prim and grim while others had a consumptive look of resignation about them. There were two favoured hair-styles. The hair was either parted in the centre and rolled into a bun on the nape of the neck or was plaited and wound round the head, like the bandeau of an Indian squaw. All wore black satin blouses and black corded jackets over a costume skirt which touched the toe-caps of their black buttoned boots. The blouses had very high-necked collars and with them they usually wore diamond-cut jet beads or cameo brooches with little watches pinned to the left side or worn on long chains round the neck.

It was only when I brought out photographs of my family and showed them off that they shyly produced theirs. They were not ashamed of their parents or their wives and daughters, but of themselves. They did not want the likeness of a wife or sister to arouse lewd thoughts in the minds of shipmates, which might be given verbal expression later, when they were not present. But few of *Lancing*'s crew were married, I think, while those that were had not seen their families for years, judging by their admissions.

Dusk found us still sailing within sight of land and we were busy now shortening down or taking in sail. We clewed up and made fast the big courses, including the foresail, and for the remainder of the night the ship sailed silently and slowly. Some of the Scottish boys chafed at the delay as they had thought that the ship should have docked and paid off on this day but they were answered by their elders with the quotation, 'Another day —another dollar!'

Shore lights were winking and flashing and we saw the clusters of lights denoting small towns and villages while those that soared skywards, dipped, flashed and disappeared we knew to be the headlights of motor cars. The night passed quietly and when daylight dawned there was Ailsa Craig, dead ahead on the surface of the misty waters, rising from the Firth like some conical sugarloaf transplanted from Rio de Janeiro. We were nearly there now!

Sailing slowly past the island we met our tug and made her fast, then we were ordered to clew up all sails for the last time. As we mounted the rigging the Second Mate let go the staysail halliards and the singing of the rattling hanks, sliding down the stays as he hauled away on the downhaul, was music in my ears.

We were all slightly intoxicated with the 'Channels' and behaved like schoolboys going on holiday. As we toiled light-heartedly on the yards a man would point to a plume of white smoke ashore and cry out, 'Hey look, there's *a train*!' Another would shout wildly and point to the nearest sandy beach in great excitement, 'Oi, look there—wimmen—swimmen!' All effort ceased while we inspected this phenomenon. A man at the bunt of a furled sail would chuckle and smack the curved lump of canvas as though it reminded him of someone. 'Won't be long now!' he would cry in savage, lustful glee.

I felt a bit downcast at all this anticipation. It was all right for them to be so happy, they were free men. But I was tied, bound hand and foot. I was going home to respectability; to church on Sundays; to meals at a dead-line; to listen to the boring, uninteresting conversation of my mother's friends and relatives; to hear my father, during meals, discuss diseases and operational surgery with Dr MacColl and to the background chatter of my four sisters, talking about their school-teachers and friends, tennis, dancing and parties!

But I soon cheered myself up. I had money coming to me and I did not need to confine myself to the house all day. The family's holidays were over, but mine were about to start. No more school now, and if I could not lay in bed late in the mornings owing to my mother's insistence on all members of the family appearing for meals promptly, I could at least stay up late for supper. Perhaps I could even wriggle out of the duty of church attendance. I had now supreme confidence in my ability to direct the course of my own future.

When my money was gone I would get another sailing ship and sail away, leaving Glasgow to its smoke and dirt, the noisy trams and grey, depressing schools and tenements and the ever-present rumble of vehicular traffic, to say nothing of these other pealing horrors which depressed my spirits to their lowest ebb once a week. The hundreds of church bells on miserable Sunday mornings and evenings, creating an atmosphere of rigid, dictatorial rectitude!

The gateway to all this was the beauty of the Firth of Clyde, through which we were now slowly towing. The green hills and the flat lands of the Ayrshire coast with its long, yellow, sandy beaches to starboard. To port were the rocky shore and steep sides of Holy Island which protects Lamlash Bay and is backed by the towering summits and deep glens of the Isle of Arran. The Cumbraes loomed ahead, but we were nearing our destination and would not pass them.

While we all stood by fore and aft, *Lancing* passed between the pier-heads and into the Eglington Tidal Basin of the Port of Ardrossan. The lock-gates ahead of the ship's bows were opened and she was towed past and into the Eglington Dock and manœuvred gently alongside the same quay, with its cranes, at the foot of Princes Street where I had joined her.

As we all worked like beavers, tying up the ship to the wharf, a thought was troubling me. I asked a shipmate, 'Will we have to stay here and work the cargo out of her?' The answer uplifted my spirits and was reassuring. 'Not bloody likely, the dockers do that. We'll be finished in half an hour and paid off by noon. Then you can go home!'

As the gangway was being lifted from the deck by the jib of a shore crane, some of us manned the braces for the last haul. We braced the yards so as to give clearance for the jibs of two cranes to swing inboard. As soon as the gangway had been made fast, and before the stanchions could be shipped on it, the dockers were streaming aboard and, with the Finnish Carpenter, were uncovering the hatches and starting to work the cargo out of her. I wished them luck for they would have to start breaking out cargo with a corkscrew!

The Chief Mate, Mr Larsen, spoke briefly to the two Bo'suns at the head of the gangway who turned away and bawled the information we had been waiting for along the waist. 'All right, that'll do the watches!' A man near me spoke. 'Finito—finish with watches—finish with ship.' And turning to some others he said, 'Tonight I be in Scotland Road, Liverpool!' He made the motion of raising a pint glass and drinking.

Returning to the shelter of the fo'c'sle deck we cleaned our hands with rags dipped into kerosene. The oil from the mooring wires had left their marks on us. I tried to clean oil stains off the front of my trouser legs but only succeeded in spreading them. Buckets and hot water were now in great demand for washing and shaving. The dockside bums had boarded the ship and moved amongst us, proffering their services as baggage-men and pimps. 'Take yer up to a wee hoose whit we jist moved intae. Lots O fine weemen wull be there. We'r all ha'en a bit o' a party. Whut d'ye say, sailor?' Or 'Whaur *ye* goin,' sailor? Och, Liverpool. A'll carry yer bag tae the station an pit it in the Left Luggage and ye can hae a wee dram on the way ower!' Some of them, to clinch a verbal contract with a particular seaman, fetched half a bucketful of hot water from the galley.

The accordion was now disposed of. On the last night at sea

it had been agreed that the instrument would be raffled but now that the ship had docked and everybody was impatient to get their money and go ashore to sample the delights awaiting them, they could not be bothered with it. Pelle put in a bid and, with the careless generosity of seamen, they said he could have it for thirty bob and he could help them spend it in the Eglington Arms Hotel!

Pelle put the cased instrument into his bunk then hurried out of the fo'c'sle to get water for a wash. He and Larvik and one or two others were remaining in the ship. I think there was some quibble with the immigration people that if they were discharged then they would have to be repatriated, so they always 'worked by' the ship until she signed on again. Pelle was a deserter from a Swedish naval school ship so he had no desire to return home. That accordion had been worth four extra men in the ship for the pleasure and happiness which it gave us all.

The Steward came forward and informed the Bo'sun that the Consul and the Shipping Master were aboard and the ship was about to pay off! Gradually we followed the line of seamen into the saloon and it was just the same as when we had signed on, even Mrs Pedersen, the Captain's wife, was sitting in the same chair and in the same position, with her head thrown back looking upwards happily, knees close together and ankles crossed under the chair while the Captain stood near her, dressed in his shore clothes and smoking the straight-stemmed and evil-smelling pipe. He, too, looked pleased.

The Consul, Shipping Master, Immigration Officer and clerks were all seated at the starboard table and there was a strong aroma of whisky in the old saloon. The Captain's family were seated to port or moving about and talking with each other.

Pound and ten-shilling notes and cylinders of silver coins were stacked in neat array on the green baize tablecloth while a dinner plate was half filled with copper coins.

The man in front of me turned away, grasping notes and silver in both hands and it was now my turn to sign my name. I picked up the discarded pen, dipping it into the small bottle of ink and as my eyes followed the pointing finger of the clerk to a line on a ledger, Mrs Pedersen spoke to me and I lost the place when answering her.

'Yes,' I said, I had enjoyed the voyage. 'Yes, I would remain at sea.' 'No, I would try to get a smaller sailing ship now.' 'Yes, I had written home from Canada.' The others behind me were becoming impatient and so was the Captain. 'Sign, boy, and collect your wages,' he ordered quietly and kindly. When I picked up a few pound notes and silver placed before me on the table and stuffed them into my pockets, I heard the clerk's voice say, '£7 18s', I was overjoyed. I had expected only about £4 10s!

I bowed to Mrs Pedersen and the other ladies and girls present while the Captain smiled, nodded and wished me 'Good luck, boy!' then amid a roar of laughter from the men and giggles from the girls as I turned away, remembering too late that I had practically no seat in my trousers, I became embarrassed and confused. Clutching the torn garment with both hands I shot out of the saloon, along the alleyway, out on to the main deck and forward to the safety of the fo'c'sle where I hurriedly donned my long oilskin coat.

I engaged a thin sandy-haired baggage man with the sad, cowed eyes of a whipped whippet and a mouth like that of a fox, who was standing on my seachest and rummaging around in my bunk searching for valuables which might have been overlooked. Just at that moment the Scottish deck boy, whom I was certain had nicked my washing and fountain pen, entered the fo'c'sle with a worried look on his face. Speaking to no one in particular he announced, 'Ma wages is no richt, a shouda got near eight pun, an they've only gied me foor pun ten!' The Farmer, who was dressed for the shore, said to him, 'Get along aft to the cabin before they close the bank, and tell them your money's not right!'

My baggage man had found a small, mastless model hull of a sailing ship, discarded on my bunk shelf and asked me, 'Ye'll no want this, it'll do fur ma waines?' When I said that I did not he stuck it in his handkerchief pocket like a cigar. I spoke to him, indicating my seabag, 'All right now, come on, I'm off!'

Saying brief good-byes to all my shipmates as I left the fo'c'sle, I followed my guide, who had the bag on his shoulder, along the now strewn and cluttered main deck, past the watercasks placed near each hatch in case of fire, past the donkeyroom with its dim interior and the muted sibilant hiss of steam, past the galley, with its glorious aromas of food cooking and the hatches from which the cargo was rising swiftly to the voices of the dockers below, the signals of the hatchman and the grating, crackling whirr of crane wires against the coamings.

As I reached the head of the gangway, abaft the main rigging on the port side, I saw the Russian coming towards me, still garbed in his faded overalls and dirty-faced. His left hand was heavily bandaged and the stains of blood were seeping through the white coverings. I felt concerned because I liked him and he had helped me on my way to becoming a seaman. He explained that his fingers had been caught in the swallow of a brace block when the yard had been trimmed for the crane jibs.

I exclaimed, 'But that was over an hour ago. Where the hell have you been?' He said that he had been taken to the officers' messroom while he received First Aid attention and had stayed there waiting to pay off. 'I pay off under protest and now I go to the hospital. My three fingers been broke, I think.' He also mentioned that Stavanger and Larvik were going with him. I advised him to get there as quickly as possible and we said good-bye, as men do who have a liking for each other, with straight looks.

We shook hands warmly and briefly then he clapped his free hand on my shoulder, saying, 'You're not afraid of work, Peasoup. You will make a good seaman, and officer too, an' if you see me when you is Captain of your own ship, you'll give me bo'sun's job, hey?' With final 'good lucks' we parted.

I followed my guide down the steep gangway and along a maze of railway tracks which led us into the North Station where I paid him off with half a crown. He spat on it and put it in his pocket then hurried back to the ship.

I swaggered up to the window of the ticket office and slammed down a pound note. 'First class single to Glasgow please!' I announced confidently. The clerk looked at me and reached for the ticket rack, then hesitated and leaning well forward looked at more of me. 'Did you say *third* class single?' he asked in a louder voice. I was patient. 'No, I want a *first* single!'

He repeated 'first single' still with a query in his voice and slowly, giving me time to change my mind or realize a mistake, he flipped the pound note away from in front of me and regretfully punched and handed me a small white ticket, then my change. He seemed prepared for an argument to develop, but I turned away and walking with a nautical roll and the supreme confidence of a surplus of money in my pocket, I went in search of a train indicator board, or a porter, for the station was almost deserted.

I was not surprised at the clerk's confusion of mind, for I was aware that I looked a strange sight. Had I been penniless I would have been ashamed of myself, but with a pocketful of money I didn't care a damn what I looked like.

On this day which crowned my adventurous endeavours, Monday the 12th day of September, 1921, and under a sweltering sun, I was clad in a long oilskin coat which was buttoned from the waist down, so as to hide my ragged indecency from the vulgar gaze. I had no bottom in my trousers and the legs were torn to below the knees. My shoes were down at heel and split across the toecaps and in addition were plentifully splashed with red lead, white and brown paint and oil from the mooring wires. This colour scheme also decorated my trousers. The aforesaid tweed cap adorned my head and it, too, had its pattern of paint. The jacket of my suit was crumpled, since I had used it as a pillow but had not had occasion to wear it very often so it was in fair shape, but was concealed by the oilskin coat.

I gave a porter a shilling to put my bag in the train and when I mentioned that I wanted a first class compartment he asked to see my ticket. I had never in my short life travelled first class on the railway, but now with my own money in my pocket I was determined to do so. I felt grand and free and careless and relaxed. This was the life for me!

Settling back into the unaccustomed comfort of cushions I luxuriated, while from time to time I stuck my head out of the window, looking for the shipmates who were bound for Liverpool and should have been on this train. No doubt the Eglington Arms Hotel had enfolded them in its cool, benevolent and noisy embrace. Then the train started with a peep, a hiss of steam and a jangling of steel chains and buffers.

I rode all the way to Glasgow in solitary dignity and comfort, musing on the various incidents of the voyage and on the welcome I would receive when I landed home. I reviewed my final hour in *Lancing*'s fo'c'sle. How everyone was excited and happy and how strange some of my shipmates appeared when they were shaved, washed and dressed for the shore. I had had to look twice in order to recognize some of them. Their feet were the focal point of my interest. I had been used to the 'clacketty-clack-clack' of wooden-soled slippers and the quiet thudding of rope-yarn soles on sail canvas uppers, that, when they were all rigged out in their shore clothes, their feet appeared uncomfortable in ordinary leather shoes and boots.

I enjoyed the rush of wind through the opened carriage windows, the sensation of swift mechanical travel, the jolting and the rocking and the grind of brakes. I listened to the long drawn-out whistle and the sudden shock and roar of a train passing in the opposite direction, the rapid 'click-click-click-click' of the spinning wheels passing over the butts of the rails and the hollow quick crash, as the train passed under a bridge. I watched the slow-spinning landscape and thoroughly enjoyed the new sensation of an old experience.

With feet resting on the opposite cushions, a cigarette alight and my oilskin coat wide open, I reviewed the small number of my girl friends and speculated on how I should fare with them, now that I was a man of experienced travel and able to pay for the things which girls enjoy.

The train steamed into the approaches of Central Station and 'jig-jig-jigged' over the points so I stood up and fastened my oilskin coat. When it finally stopped, yards away from the patent emergency buffers, I pitched my seabag on to the platform and jerked my head at a porter. 'I want a taxi!' I called. He glanced at the first class carriage I had just vacated, looked back at me and winked. 'All right, Jock,' he replied grinning.

When I handed him the first class ticket his manner changed in an instant. From then on it was, 'Yes, sir—no, sir! Been ship-wrecked, sir?' This was fine! Did I really look like that? Why he must have seen hundreds of ships' survivors pass through the station during the war. As we walked to the barrier gates I looked people straight in the eyes and silently challenged them to think as the porter did.

A taxi curved alongside us and my porter shoved the bag aboard. He said to the driver, and I made no attempt to correct him, 'Young gentleman's bin ship-wrecked!' I was going to give him a shilling but now I handed over half-a-crown and received a flood of thanks, three polite salutes and a firmly but gently closed door.

The taxi wormed its devious way through the evening rush hour traffic in the centre of the city while I gazed open-eyed through the windows. Everything looked so new but so familiar. The driver avoided the tramway routes as much as he could while I gazed at the hurrying crowds, at the smart young girls with nice shapely legs and good figures, at the people leaving their offices and shops, homeward bound like me. They would reverse the journey in the morning, however, and I was selfishly glad. I was on holiday!

The taxi stopped at the signal of a traffic policeman, then started off again too soon. With a blast of his whistle the police-man stopped it in the middle of the road while he and the driver swore at each other. The driver was threatened with prosecution but it did not appear to worry him, he gave as good as he got! In those days, motorists had not been disciplined by the law to the same extent as they are now, and, besides, the police force had had many 'a hiding' from the citizens of Glasgow. Riots were by no means uncommon when I was a boy. I had been a witness to a very big riot two years previously when troops had been brought in from over the Border and guarded the Munici-pal Buildings with machine guns. I watched pitched battles fought by hundreds of police and thousands of men in the city centre! There was plenty of spirit in the citizens then.

Traffic was piling up, whips were cracking, horns tooting and the bells of tramcars stamped on by impatient drivers' feet. When voices were added to the din the policeman ceased swearing and, with red perspiring face, told the taxi driver to, 'Get the hell out of it. I've got yer number!'

The taxi shot along George Square and turned up past the Fire Station and when it reached the High Street there was another short hold-up but I did not reckon the cost to me. I was happy with anticipation. I watched the shawled women and the lounging men and the barefoot boys and the newspaper sellers.

A cart coming down the ramp of The Union Cold Storage slid sideways as the hooves of the horse slipped and steel rang loudly, striking sparks from the stones. A little dog sniffed at the foot of a trolley wire standard, edged alongside with uplifted leg then trotted along the pavement steering 'full and by' crabwise, shaking its ears.

The taxi jerked into life and rushed down the steep hill of Duke Street, past the gloomy prison facing the goodsyard, then charged the opposite hill leading up from the dip, past the men's hostel and the brewery and levelled off at the hospital and cattle market. At Belgrove Street a familiar, big, red-faced policeman waved it on and the vehicle turned left into Westercraigs and right into Annfield Place. My suppressed excitement was now at fever heat as we coasted quietly along the cindered private road and, with a gentle sigh, stopped outside our home, No 11.

I saw faces appear at the dining-room windows, looking over the etched and frosted lower halves. The broad front door opened wide and there were all the females of the household to welcome me home. My mother, my four sisters Pearl, Eileen, Dora and Sheila, Nurse Smith and the servants.

The taxi driver, who had doubtless seen my tip to the porter or judged the amount by the man's reactions, carried my seabag into the house and deposited it in the hall. I hurriedly paid him off before he could start gossiping about some ship-wreck or other, and then I was surrounded!

I have little recollection of the conversation of the next hour except that my welcome was just as happy and eventful as I had thought it would be. I remember that my mother's face paled as I slowly removed my oilskin coat and stood revealed. She gave a horrified gasp! '*Whatever* has happened to you, Gavin? Have you injured yourself? Is that *blood* on your shoes? And just look at the state of them! What *have* you been doing?'

I explained and reassured her while my sisters choked with helpless laughter and insisted on walking round me while they remarked on how sunburned I was. My mother's habit of authority reasserted itself. 'Go straight to your room, dear, and take these *awful* clothes off. Have a good wash and change into something decent for your father will be home shortly!'

My room appeared smaller than ever now and the single bed very wide. I liked the look of clean sheets and big soft pillows and the thought of comfortable sagging springs, and waking up in these familiar and rock-steady surroundings, but I would miss the view of the sea and the fore-rigging through the port.

When I descended to the dining room, resplendent in shorts and a cricket shirt and the slippers I had managed to leave behind, I was bidden to take my seabag into the kitchen and unpack it. My mother and sisters accompanied me, foreboding showing in their faces. I did not disappoint them either.

As they all stood around watching I unlashed the bag, turned it upside down and proceeded to shake the contents on to the floor. There were exclamations of disgust as the torn and dirty garments spilled out and my seaboots clattered against the steel fender in front of the big coal-fired range.

I dropped the clean seabag on top of the tattered remains, saying lamely, 'Well, I didn't have much time to wash and mend them, you see . . .' But my excuses were cut short by a shriek from one of my sisters, 'Oh, mother, look at that thing there!' She was pointing down at the heap on the floor. Another horrified cry as another sister screamed! 'There's another one—and another!' They all backed away and tried to get behind each other. Mother cried, 'Great heavens, they're beetles. Gavin, throw these clothes out into the garden at once!' The maid said, 'Them's no beetles, Mum.' And taking off her shoe she proceeded to flatten the cockroaches to the linoleum while the cook armed herself with a shovel for the same purpose.

I carried my gear out the back door and dumped it all on the flag-stones under the kitchen and pantry windows where Bucket, the house cat, explored the pile with nervous dilated nostrils and poised paw. The slaughter had ended when I returned to the kitchen and the cook was holding a shovel while the maid swept the bodies into it with a soft broom. I hastened to explain that they were only 'jaspers' and harmless. I concluded, 'I ate one by accident during the voyage!' but I could see they did not believe me.

My father returned in due course and welcomed me with pleasure, asking, where my black bride was. It was one of his standing jokes. He forecast that I would return from some voyage bringing 'a dusky maiden home as your bride!'

We were a very happy and cheerful family round the tea table that night as I was plied with questions about my experiences in *Lancing* and in Canada. I lied about Canada and said that I had been ashore and that I liked the country very much, when in fact, all that I had seen of North America was a rocky shore, green hills and white smoke. I did not want them to think that I had been cheated, that I had sailed 5,000 miles and never set foot ashore, so to spare their feelings of sympathy for me, I lied. Dr MacColl kidded me about my experiences and he forecast that within a year or two I would have command of the *Mauretania*, or perhaps the *Aquitania*!

It was very late as I said good-night to my father, as usual the only one left before the fire, and as I made my way up the solid staircase I looked at the grandfather clock in the hallway and noticed that it was after two o'clock, I really felt adult!

The gaslight had been lit in my room by one of the servants, or perhaps by my mother, and was turned low. I turned it up brightly and looked around the small room, at the familiar chest-of-drawers on which was the model full-rigged ship in the glass case, the old and crippled armchair, in which the cat had once had kittens before my very eyes, and the seachest of Captain McKellar. I had now some real knowledge of the workings of such a ship and that of the two pictures of sailing ships which adorned the straight walls of my attic. I abstracted a pair of pyjamas and, stripping off, put them on. But shed the trousers again as they felt uncomfortable for I had no feeling of freedom, but for the sake of appearances in the morning, retained the jacket.

Obeying an inner urge, I stood on the bottom rail of my bed, as I had always done, and looked through the skylight. The early morning was clear and warm with little wind while the sky was bright with stars. I savoured the air and thought of my shipmates in Ardrossan and perhaps in Liverpool, of the ship I had left and the voyage I had made in her.

I could feel the still warm air in the room holding my body while my face, turned to the westward, was fanned by a soft breeze. I had a sense of great satisfaction over my former restlessness but I knew that my life lay beyond the nearest horizon of roof ridges and chimneys. In other ships I would go out there again and again, and with a last glance to the westward as I prepared to slide luxuriously into bed, whispered, 'I've done it, I've been out there at last!'

Lancing *ex* Pereire

Pereire

The Compagnie Générale Transatlantique (now the French Line) placed an order for two sister ships with the firm of Robert Napier & Sons, Glasgow, to the designs of Sir William Pearce, a naval architect of considerable distinction on both sides of the Channel. The keels were laid down in the year 1865. The steamships were to be built of iron, driven by paddles and rigged as brigs, but while still on the stocks, the French Line, which was keeping a close watch on the North Atlantic competition and in particular the success of Cunard's screw steamer *Scotia*, order major modifications to both ships. *Pereire* and *Ville de Paris* were given screw-populsion and rigged as barques. For some reason, the latter vessel was about 135 tons larger than the former.

The eminent French nautical historian, Contre-Amiral Marcel J. Adam, CVO, CBE, writes of *Pereire*, that her dimensions were: length overall 113·38m; breadth 13·33m; depth 8·85m; gross tonnage 3,015; deadweight 1,916; draught 6·90m. Her power came from a two-cylinder vertical engine of 3,390 ihp; she had four double and two single boilers 4 kgs/cm², giving 15·35 knots. Both vessels designed as passenger ships with 226 berths in the first class, 98 in the second and 31 in the third.

The Admiral states that on *Pereire*'s maiden voyage from Havre to New York in 1866, she completed the passage in ten days, cutting this on the following voyage to nine days. He goes on, 'During her 1872/73 refit at Govan by Napier's, her engines were compounded with the addition of an hp cylinder in front of the others, and she received new boilers. This is when she was given two funnels in place of the single. At this time her horse power was stepped up from 900 to 1,250.'

The closing years of *Pereire* would appear to have included Mediterranean voyages. While on passage from Marseilles to Malta in the year 1881 she experienced machinery trouble and put in to Goletta in the Gulf of Tunis. While at anchor a fire started and it must have got out of control for the French Navy was called in and scuttled the ship by means of a spar-torpedo. This is an obsolete weapon which consisted of a torpedo war-head fixed to the outer end of a long spar projecting from the bow of a steam launch; the method of attack was by direct ramming. Since the *Pereire*'s shell plating was two inches thick it is no wonder that they had to resort to such drastic methods.

In the year 1888 the *Pereire* was put on the sale list (together with her sister). Who actually purchased both ships is unknown but they were converted by the firm of Blyth Dry Docks Company of Blyth. It may well be that this firm invested in the two hulls as a speculation; however, it is known that *Pereire* fetched 54,800 francs, minus engines and boilers. The conversions were made at a berth in the Flanker at Blyth, and both vessels were rigged as four-masted full-rigged ships.

I have been unable to trace the origin of the name *Lancing* in spite of intensive research. Little information regarding her career survived the Second World War but it is possible to trace the highlights from the brief writings of historians and interested seafarers in such journals as *Sea Breezes*, the *Journal of Commerce* and extracts from newspapers of the day.

When converted to a sailing ship the iron foremast was shifted aft and became the jigger mast, while the three new masts and most of the yards were constructed of steel. The fo'c'sle deck-house was constructed of teak, similar to the poop deck-house, and this fo'c'sle had formed part of a second class dining saloon, which explains the square ports in the afterpart. I have reason to believe that the iron deck-house, containing the galley, donkey boiler and bilge tank pump, was part of the original fiddley. The flat-topped hold ventilators on the main-deck were, I think, the shafts of the cowl ventilators which originally passed through the deck-house, fore and aft, serving the passenger accommodation in the 'tweendecks.

Lloyds Register of the years 1921/22 has the following entry:

Lancing 356′ 0″ × 43′ 8″ × 27′ 3″ $\frac{2785—2546}{2622}$ $\frac{100\ AI}{12—20}$ *Christiania*

Her plans show a long, narrow vessel of about eight and a half beams to the length, with a fine hollow entrance and a long tapering run. The bottom plating amidships from the big bar keel to the bilge strake was the reverse to that in clipper ship design since it described a convex curve as opposed to the usual concave. No bilge keels were fitted, and as she was of iron construction her shell plating was long and narrow, while she had practically no sheer and little tumblehome. Her block co-efficient was ·62. (For comparison Donald MacCulloch quotes the block coefficient of *Cutty Sark* ·55, *Herzogin Cecilie* ·78, *Preussen* ·81 and *France* ·82.)

The ballast tanks were of great benefit. They had a maximum depth of 10 feet 6 inches and were eight in number, No. 8 being used for fresh water. They occupied a length of 122 feet. No wood ceilings were laid in the holds, and she was not fitted with wood stringers or battens in holds or 'tweendecks.

When fully rigged, the main and mizzen masts measured 203 feet from keelson to truck and 175 feet from the main deck. The main and mizzen yards were reported to be 98 feet 9 inches in length. A full set of square and fore-and-aft sails numbered 36 with a total sail area of close on two acres; the mainsail alone had 5,200 square feet of canvas. Her standing and running rigging measured 30 miles in total length.

Presumably because of the fire and salvage, she had no laid wood deck amidships and because of this she was known to seafarers the world over as, 'The ship with the iron deck'. She was unique in several respects. She carried her name twice on each bow; on the decorative trailboards, and again on the bluff of the bow in larger letters below the fore rigging.

Owing to the absence of a laid-deck the bulwarks were higher than is usual, so small Jacob's ladders were fitted to give access to the rigging, two to each gang of shrouds, except in the fore rigging which had only one, as most of the lower rigging set up on the fo'c'sle-head.

Her high bulwarks had a certain interest for their height was greatest from the break of the poop to the mizzen backstays where they dropped about ten inches in a break or 'drift' similar to that in the New England fishing schooners. The space between the mainrail and the t'gallant cap rail, throughout this length only, was decorative wooden panelling. Presumably the extra height was to give shelter to the first class passengers and their top-hats, as they took a turn or two along the length of the quarterdeck alleyways. The decorative panels emphasized that this section of the ship had more luxury than appeared elsewhere, which induced the belief that they were getting their money's worth. No doubt the gilt carving, the smooth varnish, the clean smooth decks and the spotless white paintwork won the approval of the Emperor Napoleon III when he visited *Pereire* unexpectedly in the port of Le Havre on June 21st, 1867.

After conversion to a sailing ship, she was remarkable for the small amount of leeway she made when beating to windward. In fact, her wake actually streamed to leeward until the foresail was taken in. After that she performed in similar manner to all other sailing ships.

Some of the former first class staterooms were in her until she was broken up. They were used as a lazarette and hospital under the saloon deck-house. I worked in these dungeons for about half-an-hour and it was like being in another ship, in another age.

Curiously, when converted, the propeller aperture was left open and when she made the passage down the North Sea to load in London, great difficulty was experienced with the steering, so she had to put into a Channel port to have the aperture filled in and plated over. Presumably this was when she was given an extension to the rudder blade.

So far as is known, her first owner was G. A. Hatfield of Yarmouth, Nova Scotia, and it is said she was commanded by him and others of the family; but the ship was actually purchased by the firm of Kinnear & Co., London, which managed her for Hatfield.

The ship changed hands several times after the Hatfields had her; she also changed her flags. From being a Canadian 'bluenose' she was sold in 1893 to Johan Bryde of Sandefjord, Norway, and changed her flag again when purchased by F. Ross of Quebec, Canada. In 1901 she reverted to Norwegian

ownership becoming the property of a firm styling itself, Act.
Lancing, Johansen & Co. of Kristiania, which was her owner
until she was sold to Melsom & Melsom also of Kristiania,
about 1920.

She was finally disposed of to an Italian shipbreaking firm
in 1925 for a sum reported to be in the region of £6,250 (a
good price at that time) after a period laid up in the Gareloch.
Loaded with coal, an Italian master and crew sailed her out
to Genoa where, after discharge, she was towed to Savona
on April 8th and steered on to the mudflats.

Pereire's sister ship, *Ville de Paris*, was also converted into a
four masted full-rigged ship at the same time and place. She,
however, profited by the steering trouble of *Lancing*, and had
her propeller aperture plated over before putting to sea. She
was sold to a firm in Bremen and renamed *H. Bischoff*. She made
no name for herself as a sailer, and was wrecked by stranding
in the River Elbe in October, 1900.

This book is a farewell to a great ship. Also to the many fine
seamen of all ranks and capacities who sailed her with respect
under the flags she wore with dignity and grace throughout
the oceans and ports of the world, for twenty-three years as a
transatlantic mail and passenger steamer besides a further
thirty-seven years as a commercial sailing ship. She retained
a 100 A1 Classification at Lloyd's to the end of her life of sixty
years of active participation. Her last record!

OUTSTANDING RECORDS

The ship made many records, some of which have
never been equalled by any other sailing vessel of any
tonnage or rig. They have been checked by Captain
Chris Steenstrupt, who at the time of my research
had access to the incomplete log-books in the Norwegian Maritime Museum at Oslo.

Atlantic crossing, west to east, Sandy Hook to Orkney Islands.
6 days, 18 hours (1916)

Newcastle, N.S.W., to San Francisco, U.S.A.   56 days (1901)

St. John, New Brunswick, to Melbourne, Australia.   79 days (1907)

Kristiania, Norway, to Melbourne, Australia (having had to beat against a strong head wind in the North Sea for five days.   74 days

On a passage from Rio de Janeiro to Nouméa, New Caledonia, her average speed was $12\frac{1}{2}$ knots. She travelled at a speed of 18 knots, by patent log measurement, for 72 consecutive hours with the wind unsteady, sometimes hauling from abeam, to aft on either quarter. The ship logged 21 knots during several watches.

Another record is 22 knots, by patent log, for 15 consecutive hours, while 'running her easting down' on a passage to Melbourne. This has never been equalled and stands today (1970) as the sailing ship world record.   (1890/91)

The ship beat the Danish mail steamer R.M.S. *Frederick VIII* by one whole day on a passage from New York, U.S.A., to Aarhus, Denmark, in 20 days.   (1917)

Other notable passages are:

Matane, Quebec Province, Canada, to Queenstown, Ireland. 14 days (1910)

Leith, Scotland, to Valparaiso, Chile.   90 days (1915)

Antofagasta, Chile, to New York, U.S.A.   77 days (1915)

Aarhus, Denmark, to Halifax, Nova Scotia.   22 days (1916)

Halifax, Nova Scotia, to Greenock, Scotland.   15 days (1916)

Santos, Brazil, to Melbourne, Australia.   46 days (1918)

Melbourne to Barbados, West Indies.   69 days (1918)

New Orleans, U.S.A., to Queenstown, Ireland.   30 days (1918)

Greenock, Scotland, to Buenos Aires, Argentina. 41 days (1920)

Cape Chat, Quebec Province, to Ardrossan, Scotland. 16 days (1921)

Within 12 months the ship completed four round voyages across the Atlantic, including loading and discharging times.

Crew List of *Lancing*, July 1921

HYREOPGJOR for   4/m. Skib. " Lancing "   af Chr

Ardrossan, Cap-Chat og Ardrossan,

...gedag i   Ardrossan   9/7-21   ...til Udløsningsdag i   Ardrossan 30/9-21

Nr.	NAVN OG STILLING.	fra og med.	til og med.	Tid ialt.	@ per Maaned.	Ialt optjent Hyre, paa denne Reise Kr.	Ore	£	s.	D.
1.	P.Th.Pedersen Fører,	10/7	30/9	2.m.21	100	270	-			
2.	A.Larsen Styrmand	"	"	" " "	500	1383	33			
3.	J.Hansen 2.den de	"	1/10	2 - 22	400	1095	34			
4.	H.Fjeldmand Letmatros	"	30/29	2 - 21	200	553	33			
5.	K.A.Andreasen Stuert	"	1/10	2 - 22	500	1400	00			
6.	E. Engeborg Kok	"	"	" "	300	852	85			
7.	A. Sørensen Letm.	"	"	"	200	560	00			
8.	G. Thjømø Gut/				90	252	00			
9.	T. Torkildsen Baasmand	11/7	13/9	2 " 3	270	567	00			
10.	F. De Vries Donkeym.	"	"	" " "	"	567	00			
11.	E. Skog Sailm.	"	"	" " "	280	588	00			
12.	W Taylor Mat.	"	"	" " "	260	546	00			
13.	B. Yarvinen "	"	"	" " "	260	546	00			
14.	K. Matsen. "	"	1/10	2 " 21	260	702	00			
15.	W. Mickelsen "	"	13/9	2 " 3	260	546	00			
16.	A. Sjoblon "	"	"	" " "	260	546	00			
17.	M. Schultz "	"	"	" " "	260	546	00			
18.	T. Lea "	"	"	" " "	260	546	00			
19.	W. Tromelås "	"	"	" " "	260	546	00			
20.	V. Bethel "	"	"	" " "	260	546	00			
21.	K. Kristoffersen Mat.	"	"	" " "	260	546	00			
22.	J. Newling	"	"	" " "	175	567	50			
23.	E. Newling Letm.	"	"	" " "	100	210	00			
24.	G. Craig "	"	"	" " 6	90	198	00			
A.	Robertson "	"	"	" " "	150	330	00			
26.	G. Baird "	"	"	" " "	100	220	00			
27.	G. Cumming "	"	"	" " "	100	220	00			
						1522 6	83			
	Afbetalt Cap-Chat									
	G. Matsen. Mat.	11/7	20/8	1m 10	110;-	400	00	13	6	8
	— Overtid					925	38	129		
	Overtid									
						Kr. 1652 41				

Ardrossan 3/10-21.
P.Th.Pedersen
Fører,

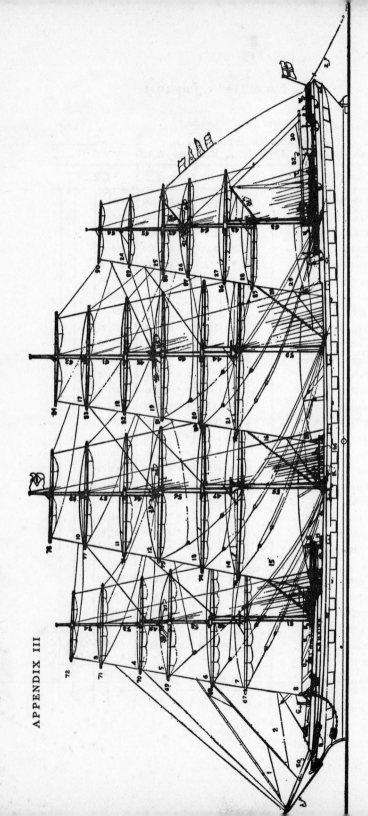

APPENDIX III

Lancing

Sails 1 to 30

1 Jib (partly obscured)
2 Fore topmast staysail (partly obscured)
3 Fore royal

73 Mainyard
74 Main lower topsail yard
75 Main upper topsail yard
76 Main lower topgallant yard

7 Fore lower topsail
8 Foresail (or fore-course)
9 Main topmast staysail (partly obscured)
10 Main royal
11 Main upper topgallant sail
12 Main lower topgallant sail
13 Main upper topsail
14 Main lower topsail
15 Mainsail (or main-course)
16 Mizzen topmast staysail (partly obscured)
17 Mizzen royal
18 Mizzen upper topgallant sail
19 Mizzen lower topgallant sail
20 Mizzen upper topsail
21 Mizzen lower topsail
22 Mizzen (or mizzen-course)
23 Jigger topmast staysail (partly obscured)
24 Jigger royal
25 Jigger upper topgallant sail
26 Jigger lower topgallant sail
27 Jigger upper topsail
28 Jigger lower topsail
29 Crossjack or 'Crojik' (jigger-course)
30 Spanker (or Driver)

Mast and Spar Arrangement

31 Spanker gaff ('sliding'—*up and down*—as opposed to the usual 'fixed' or standing-gaff type)
32 Spanker boom
33 Signal gaff (or monkey-gaff)
34 Spreaders (port and starboard)
35 "   "   "   "
36 "   "   "   "

38 Crosstrees
39 "
40 "
41 "
42 Mast doublings
43 "   "   "
44 "   "   "
45 "   "   "
46 "   "   "
47 "   "   "
48 "   "   "
49 "   "   "
50 Bowsprit
51 Fore lowermast
52 Fore topmast
53 Fore topgallant mast
54 Fore royal mast (and royal pole)
55 Main lowermast
56 Main topmast
57 Main topgallant mast
58 Main royal mast (and royal pole)
59 Mizzen lowermast
60 Mizzen topmast
61 Mizzen topgallant mast
62 Mizzen royal mast (and royal pole)
63 Jigger lowermast
64 Jigger topmast
65 Jigger topgallant mast
66 Jigger royal mast (and royal pole)
67 Foreyard
68 Fore lower topsail yard
69 Fore upper topsail yard
70 Fore lower topgallant yard
71 Fore upper topgallant yard
72 Fore royal yard

80 Mizzen lower topsail yard
81 Mizzen upper topsail yard
82 Mizzen lower topgallant yard
83 Mizzen upper topgallant yard
84 Mizzen royal yard
85 Crossjack yard (or 'Crojik' yard)
86 Jigger lower topsail yard
87 Jigger upper topsail yard
88 Jigger lower topgallant yard
89 Jigger upper topgallant yard
90 Jigger royal yard
A Bobstay (iron bar)
B Bowsprit guys (steel wire rope)
C Anchor crane (partly obscured)
D Capstan
E Fore hatch
F Steam cargo winch
G Longboat and pram dinghy (both inverted)
H Forecastle deck-house (wooden)
J Ship's bell, for timing, and transmitting signals
K Midship deck-house (iron) contains donkey boiler and ballast pump
M Galley—after end of deck-house
N Lifeboats (port and starboard)
P Bridge ladders, placed athwartships
R After deck-house (poop extension)
S Captain's entrance
T Saloon skylight
V Poop ladder, in athwartship's alleyway
W Sunken wheelhouse
X Full poop, half-round
Z Logline, measures distance travelled through water (not 'over the ground')

Standing Rigging

This is shown on the diagram sketch but is not numbered or named, for clarity. Stays are single or double wire ropes which support the masts in a fore and aft direction on the centreline and lead from the bowsprit, the decks and the backs of masts, to various positions on the front of each section of all masts. The triangular staysails which were set on these stays were named after the section of mast which the stays supported, with the exception of the jibs.

Shrouds and backstays support the masts on each side of the ship. They are secured close to the deck and lead upwards to various positions on each section of all masts. Their positions, number and lead is shown by broken lines, except for the royal backstays. No topgallant shrouds or ratlines (wooden battens forming a ladder on the shrouds) are shown, for clarity.

Running Rigging

This is composed of pliable manila ropes and wire ropes which lead from wood or iron belaying pins inside the bulwarks and around the masts, through arrangements of blocks (pulleys) and so to their destination on the sails or yards. Their purpose is to furl the sails, and hoist, lower and swing the yards from side to side. Those which furl the sails have the names *buntlines, clewlines, spilling lines* while those which move the yards are called *halliards, braces, downhauls* and *lifts*. In addition, every sail is fitted with two sheets, one on each lower corner or clew and the big courses have two 'tacks' to supplement the sheets. These are simply additional sheets and are sometimes used as such. Their function is the same, to hold and control the clews or lower corners. Only the braces and some sheets are shown on the sketch, and the spanker gaff halliards, vang and boom-lift. None are named.

All braces are attached to each yardarm. The lead-blocks on the three lower braces are shackled to bumkins* projecting outboard from the ship's side and the single hauling-part of each brace pass through brass-lined slots in the bulwarks to their respective belaying pins on the mainrail. All braces above them lead to the adjacent mast then down to their pins on deck. They can easily be traced on the drawing.

* Bumkin or boomkin. *This is a forged iron bar projecting at*

198

right angles to the shell plating of the hull and is fitted with three ring-projections to which the brace blocks are shackled. It is also fitted with a restraining chain. The bar is hinged in a socket on the ship's side and can be folded back when the braces are slack in port. The use of six bumkins was old style, traditional. Modern steel ships used only two, for mizzen braces. Their other lead-blocks were fixed on the mainrail inboard.